An Poc ar Buile
THE LIFE & TIMES OF
Seán Ó Sé

Ó Sé is a renowned Irish traditional singer and former
...nary school teacher. He has performed all over the world
... is particularly well known for his recording of '*An Poc
...uile*' and for his collaboration with Seán Ó Riada. Born
...llylickey near Bantry in County Cork, he lived most of
...e in Cork city, where he still resides today.

...RICIA **Ahern** is the co-author of *The Loneliest Boy in the
...rld*, *The Lightkeeper* and *In Search of the Missing*. Born in
...Mallow, she now lives in Ballinhassig, County Cork.

This book is dedicated to
Eileen, Áine and Íde, Con and Caitríona,
Méabh, Seán and Ciara.

AN POC AR BUILE
THE LIFE & TIMES OF
SEÁN Ó SÉ

SEÁN Ó SÉ
with PATRICIA AHERN

The Collins Press

FIRST PUBLISHED IN 2015 BY
The Collins Press
West Link Park
Doughcloyne
Wilton
Cork

A catalogue record for this book is available from the British Library

Paperback ISBN: 9781848892538
PDF eBook ISBN: 9781848895027
EPUB eBook ISBN: 9781848895003
Kindle eBook ISBN: 9781848895010

Typesetting by Carrigboy Typesetting Services
Typeset in Adobe Garamond Pro
Printed in Poland by Drukarnia Skleniarz

Contents

Ar scáth a chéile a mhaireann na daoine
People live in each other's shelter

(Irish proverb)

FOREWORD

Seán Ó Sé: The Voice of the People
Úna agus an Seanadóir Labhrás Ó Murchú

The story of Seán Ó Sé, the singer and raconteur, spans over a half century. During this time Ireland experienced many changes which saw the fledgling state transformed into a confident and progressive entity, having taken its place among the nations of the world. Our cultural identity, though challenged and at times eroded, remained intact. Then a new generation of young Irelanders took on the task of redeeming and enhancing our cultural treasures. Seán Ó Sé played a pivotal role in this cultural renaissance.

As a proud son of Munster and a dedicated teacher, the young Cork Gael set himself firmly on the journey of Davis, Pearse and Ó Riada. His singing – full of feeling, passion, reverence and, yes, patriotism – carried with it an echo of the noble and Gaelic Ireland, full of promise and creativity.

Seán Ó Sé traversed and explored the Irish psyche, ever conscious of our history of survival and determination to sustain those characteristics which set us apart as a significant and ancient nation. Seán drew sustenance from the well of tradition which was to be found in the Gaeltacht or wherever the Gaeil foregathered in celebration of who we are as a people.

His songs spoke of valiant deeds and noble aspirations. When delivered by the master, which was Seán Ó Sé, these songs inspired young and old with a sense of national pride and tenacity of character. Whether on a stage in an Irish rural setting or on a world stage, Seán spoke to the hearts which yearned for a voice to tell their story and claim their cultural inheritance. This he did with a sense of duty and privilege and in a manner that left an abiding message which lingered well into the future. He sowed the seed for others to harvest.

Seán Ó Sé never forgot his roots. He is truly a man of the people, sharing their joys and sorrows, whether they were hurlers playing the sliothar on the green sod of Ireland; or craftsmen, musicians, poets, and those who stood their ground for human rights and values.

People will celebrate Seán's outstanding talents as a performer and reflect on his generosity in sharing those talents with so many at home and abroad. Brú Ború and Comhaltas Ceoltóirí Éireann can attest to this generosity – he has travelled with us and cheered us on many a fruitful journey. He lifted our spirits and helped us raise the flag to the top of the mast.

Seán Ó Sé's cultural journey has brought him from Cork to Cuba; from Cashel to China; from Armagh to America; from Mayo to Moscow; and so many other destinations in between. He crafted enduring designs and colours in a comforting tapestry which embraced all men and women of goodwill who shared their dreams and achievements in a fraternal global celebration. Yes, he is a singer par excellence but he is also a leader, an ambassador and one who is a beacon in the choppy and turbulent seas of change. His message and his talents have stood the test of time and are still vibrant and relevant to this very day.

With heartfelt pride, affection and appreciation we salute this man who has raised a pedestal for others to occupy. It has been a wonderful experience as we travelled together, carried on high by an all embracing patriotism, adding to the story of Ireland in all her splendid grandeur. Seán, *ní dhéanfar dearmad riamh ort an fhaid is a bheidh Gael fágtha in Éirinn.*

Do sheas tú an fód linn, a Sheáin. Do thug tú misneach agus bród dúinn. Do spreag tú sinn in am an gháthair. Do shiúil tú linn ar an ród a bhí romhainn. Tá clú agus cáil tuillte go maith agat. Gura fada buan tú.

PROLOGUE

Shortly after singing for President de Valera, Pádraig Tyers, who managed the Cork office of Gael Linn, suggested that I should send a demo tape to the Gael Linn headquarters in Dublin, with a view to making a record. Immediately, I thought of the song I had heard Dónal Ó Mulláin sing all those years ago in Coláiste Íosagáin, '*An Poc ar Buile*'.

As it happened, the harpist and singer Deirdre Ní Fhloinn was living in Cork at the time. She was a most generous and helpful person and with her help we made a demo tape of '*An Poc ar Buile*'.

Gael Linn always did great work in recording Irish traditional singers and I hoped against hope that they might include me among their recording artists. The man with the power to decide this was the deputy director of Gael Linn, Roibeárd MacGabhráin, whom I knew through the Gael Linn Cabaret. After sending off the demo, word quickly came back that Roibeárd was indeed in favour of recording '*An Poc ar Buile*'.

On the following Saturday, Roibeárd invited me along to his home in Stillorgan in Dublin to audition for Seán Ó Riada, to see if he would have any interest in producing the proposed record. By then, Seán Ó Riada was famous as the composer of the music for *Mise Éire*, the documentary film by George Morrison about the 1916 Rising and the founding of the Republic of Ireland.

Shortly after I landed at Roibeárd's house, a big, green Jaguar pulled up outside. Seán Ó Riada stepped out, with his hair tossing in the wind, smoke rising from a big cigar and a gabardine raincoat tightly belted around his waist. Roibeárd led him inside and introduced him to me. While I was delighted and excited to meet him, I was extremely nervous about auditioning for such a great composer and musician.

The audition went well and so began my singing career in earnest.

1

A Child of War and Peace

When I was a child, I was very shy and felt out of the loop with other boys, maybe because both my parents were teachers in the school I attended. Yet, in later years, when it came to belting out a verse of a song, my shyness never held me back. Instead, it spurred me on to sing, as it was only when I sang that I really came out of myself.

But it was natural that I should sing, as singing was in my blood, going way back through the generations. My grandfather Con O'Shea was known for his love of singing. Originally from Kerry, he was born at the top of Glanmore Lake, at the foot of the famous Tim Healy Pass, in 1845 at the time of the Famine. Later in life, he crossed over the Pass from Glanmore and settled on the Beara Peninsula in Adrigole, on the southwest coast of Ireland. In time, he bought a small farm there. He met and married Catherine O'Sullivan from Trafrask, a neighbouring townland. Together they had nine children, four boys and five girls. As well as farming the land

and mending shoes – he was a cobbler – he 'carred' butter in his pony and trap to the butter market in Cork city for neighbouring farmers who buried firkins of butter in a bog until there was a load of them ready for my grandfather to take to Cork. In its day, that market – situated in the shadow of Shandon Steeple and known as the Firkin Crane – was the largest butter market in the world and so important that it set the price of butter all over Europe.

After dropping off his load, my grandfather always stayed overnight at the bottom of Shandon Street in a licensed lodging house – or doss house as it was called then – known as The Rookery. There, he mingled, drank and sang with men from all parts of the country and listened to their songs. Mostly, they sang traditional songs, both in English and Irish. His return home was eagerly awaited and on his arrival all work ceased and the family gathered round him, hoping that he would have new songs for them, which they could add to their repertoire. He rarely disappointed them.

Like my grandfather, many of his nine children were good singers, among them my aunts Mary and Siobhán, my father Con, who was the youngest, and my uncle Mort, who was also a great footballer and often cycled from Adrigole to Cork city to play with the Lees football club, the players of which were mainly country boys working in Cork. In 1911, Mort won an All-Ireland senior football medal with Cork – a rare feat for a Corkman in those days. My father was a talented footballer too and happened to be picked to play for Waterford against Cork in the first round of the 1911 championship. But the rules of

Sean's father's family, taken at home in Adrigole around 1910, (*l–r*): Seán's aunts Nora and Kate, his grandfather Con, uncle Mort, grandmother Catherine, cousin Eamonn (youngest child of Seán's aunt Julia), father Con and aunts Mary and Siobhán.

the college he was attending at the time prevented him from taking part. And so he missed out on playing against Mort. From about 1915 to 1921, my father played with the Cork senior football team. He was reputed to be a handy corner forward and won a medal with the Bantry Blues senior football team in 1913, when they won the Kelleher Shield trophy after taking part in the competition for the first time.

Of the O'Shea family, my father and his siblings were the first generation to get second level education. Such progress may be credited to my grandmother, Catherine, who was a very competent and shrewd woman. Her people were reputed to be distant relatives of the five famous Sullivan brothers, who joined the American navy and whose ship was sunk and lost in the Second World War. Later, they became known as the Fighting Sullivans and were recently commemorated in Adrigole when an American destroyer named in their honour visited Adrigole Harbour.

When my grandparents married, they lived for some time in a small building, little better than a cowshed. Eventually, they built a house there and my grandmother opened up a small grocery shop. The local doctor rented a room in the house for his dispensary and the shop did well from the trade brought in by his patients.

No doubt, the money from the shop helped with the family's education, including the education of my father Con. In 1910, he went from primary school to the De La Salle teacher training college in Waterford, where he stayed for two years until he qualified. Afterwards, he spent the first twelve years of his teaching career on Whiddy Island, which he always spoke about with great affection. While living on the island, he fished a lot with the O'Driscoll family and became engaged to one of the daughters. But the engagement didn't last. In 1924,

Con and Peig O'Shea, Seán's parents, on their wedding day, 29 January 1935, in Wren's Hotel, Pembroke Street, Cork.

he took up the post of principal at Coomhola Boys' National School, 5 miles from Bantry.

Like my father, my mother Margaret Twomey, who was known to most as Peig, especially in her childhood, came from a big family. Her parents and their eight children lived in the last house in the parish of Bantry, towards Céim an Fhia, and barely eked out a living on their small farm. Sadly, Mam's mother was delicate for a long time and died at an early age. After her passing, my great-grandmother took over the care of the children. She was a native speaker and spoke to them only in Irish, the one language she knew.

At school, my mother had a wonderful teacher from Tournafulla in County Limerick called Willie Island O'Sullivan. One evening, he took her aside and said, 'Maggie, your best chance in life is your books, girl.' She heeded his words and never looked back. At the age of thirteen, she won a scholarship to a secondary school in Arklow. After finishing there, she took up a post in Bantry convent as a monitor, or trainee teacher. Then, in 1920, she headed to Belfast, where she trained as a teacher at St Mary's College.

By 1924, when my father took over as principal at Coomhola Boys' National School, my mother was already teaching there. In no time at all, a romance between them blossomed. I believe one of their favourite pastimes was roaming the country together on my father's motor bike, a BSA, made by the Birmingham Small Arms Company. But my mother was slow to marry, as she got a cancer scare early in life and felt it would be best not to wed. However, in 1935, after going out with my father for eleven years, she finally gave in. At the time of their marriage, my mother was thirty-five and my father was eight years older. By a strange coincidence, on that very same day in Ballymacoda parish church near Youghal, a Kerryman called Denis Tangney married a local woman named Mary Bridget Colbert. They became the parents of my future wife Eileen.

On 16 January 1936, I was born in Cork in Mrs Harvey's Nursing Home on the South Terrace. It was a windy, frosty night when my father came to bring my mother and myself home to Ballylickey. At Innishannon, the car skidded and made a full turn around for Cork, which may have been a sign that it was there my future lay. Three years later, my sister Maureen came along. On the night my mother walked in the door with Maureen in her arms, I wasn't at all happy, as I felt my territory was being invaded. I'm told I kicked up a big tantrum and threatened to harm my baby sister if my mother didn't send her back straight away. But my mother calmed me down and over time I grew to love having Maureen around and being her big brother.

We lived in Laharn, near Ballylickey Bridge, 3 miles west of Bantry. My father had built a two-storey house there for a contract price of £900, on a one-acre site he bought for £50 from a neighbouring farmer, Connie Manning. At the time, my father earned a yearly salary of about £176. Designed by John Paul Crowley, an architect from Skibbereen, the house was typical of many houses in west Cork, with three windows above and a bay window at either side of the front door. My mother loved those bay windows and took great pride in them, especially in the summer as they gave a wonderful view of Bantry Bay.

The first important decision my parents made about raising me was that we would speak only Irish. They had both come from Irish-speaking homes, although my father's family used English too. When I started school at the age of six, being unable to speak English posed a big problem for me. But I listened hard and soon picked it up. Later, my parents decided it was more practical to talk in both Irish and English at home and so we became a bilingual family. But the early years when we spoke all Irish has left me with a great *grá* for the language.

At school, I found it hard enough to fall in with the other boys, maybe because my parents were the teachers there. None of the boys ever gave out about my parents in front of me or teased me about being their son. Then again, my parents treated me like the rest of their pupils. When it came to corporal punishment, they never excluded me. Indeed, sometimes I was included when I felt I didn't deserve to be.

Yet, even if my parents had not been teaching in the school, I may still have found it hard to fit in, as I was very shy. My shyness might have stemmed from the fact that my mother had always been over-protective of me, perhaps because when she was pregnant with me she had to spend the entire nine months in Mrs Harvey's Nursing Home in Cork city trying to hold on to me. She never liked to see me playing football in case I got hurt. After my father found some pupils smoking behind a bush in the schoolyard one day, my mother became even more vigilant about making sure that I didn't fall in with

Seán in his father's arms, aged eighteen months, June 1937, in front of the family home near Ballylickey, west Cork.

the wrong crowd. Even today, my shyness can hit me in the most unexpected places, such as walking into a room full of people. Yet, having parents as teachers had its benefits too, as my father sometimes helped me with my homework and if I did well during an inspector's visit I was usually rewarded with an ice cream. On the other hand, if I had a bad day at school, I got another telling off when I went home.

Next door to our school was the Coomhola National School for girls. Marcella Keohane was its principal. In her youth, Marcella was famous as one of the finest singers of her day. She sang traditional songs in both Irish and English and was known nationally as '*Smóilín na Mún*' – 'The Song Thrush of Munster'. Her Assistant was Katie Bracken, whose son Eddie was in the class ahead of me in the boys' school. Katie was a kind, gentle lady and one of the best Irish speakers I ever heard. My mother and herself were great friends.

When it came to teaching, my mother was very strict, unlike my father, who was more relaxed and more popular than my mother. She took no nonsense. But it was all done in the interest of her pupils and probably reflected her own situation when she was young. She wanted everyone to work hard and to make the most of their education, as she knew only too well that the opportunities around Coomhola were few and far between, except perhaps for those who might inherit a farm. Because of her drive and dedication, teaching must have caused her a lot of stress and I rarely saw the soft side of her until many years later. My mother taught all classes from junior infants up to second class and my father taught the rest. Although my father held the title of school principal, in reality I think my mother ran the show.

At that time, the school curriculum placed much importance on what was known as the three Rs (reading, writing and arithmetic) and less emphasis on geography, history and music. The history syllabus was biased in Ireland's favour, perhaps because nationalism was still very much to the fore, with the Anglo-Irish Treaty having been signed only about twenty years before.

After leaving school, most of the pupils of my time did well. Some became guards, post office clerks and teachers. Two of them became religious Brothers and later provincials in their orders, while another pair became great musicians and joined Bantry's famous Regal Showband. Many others stayed at home on the land.

At home, my mother loved treating her friend Katie Bracken to high tea in the dining room. Before eating, they always chatted for a while in the sitting room and my mother would call Maureen and me in to meet Katie, who would look us up and down and express her surprise at how much we'd grown since her last visit. Then my mother would ask us to sing a song and Katie would praise us to the hilt.

In those days, Christmas time was the highlight of each year. Unlike the Christmas of today, Christmas then was much more about celebrating the birth of the baby Jesus with much less emphasis laid on the commercial side of matters. The build-up began about two weeks before Christmas, when we put up the Christmas tree. We stood it into a bucket of earth and decorated it with cotton-wool, coloured paper and small sprigs of red-berry holly.

More than anything else, the glow of the Christmas candles always fascinated me. We lit a candle in every window and their flickering shadows brought a special magic to each room in the house. Every night after tea, I ran upstairs to look out at all the candles shimmering in the windows of the other houses around. Each house stuck to the tradition of lighting the candles for seven nights: Christmas Eve; Christmas Day; St Stephen's night; New Year's Eve; New Year's Day; the eve of the Epiphany; and the following night. Years later, when I was flying into Las Vegas and gazed at the gleaming strip below, it struck me that, despite all its beauty, it failed to match the magic of the Christmas candles in Ballylickey.

Every Christmas, we set aside a special day for Christmas shopping. We always referred to that day as just 'The Christmas'. We bought turkey, ham and a Christmas cake. Some of the shops gave presents to their regular customers and Cotter's Bakery always gave us a big barmbrack and a calendar.

On Christmas Eve, Maureen and I hung our stockings at the end of our beds for Santa, excited beyond belief at the thought of what he might bring. Then, we hopped under the bedclothes and tried our best to stay awake. Every now and then, my father peeped in to see if we were asleep. Each Christmas without fail, Santa brought me a holy book telling all about Christmas. Usually, I got a train or a bus too, a small ball and some clothes and once a lovely leather football. All too soon, Christmas ended and a new school term began.

Even before I started school, I knew that there was fighting going on between England and Germany. I knew that it was called the Second World War and that thousands of people were being killed every day in places far away from where we lived. As well as that, I knew that we had a scarcity of butter and that tea and sugar were rationed because of the war. Sometimes, my mother showed me pictures of bananas and promised me that she would get me one when the war ended. The use of private cars was restricted too, with most cars being put off the road, apart from those driven by the doctor, the parish priest, the school inspector, the Local Defence Forces officer and some taxi drivers. Newspapers had only one sheet and no photos.

During the war, our main source of entertainment was the radio, which was powered by a wet and a dry battery. We treasured that radio like nothing else we owned and used it sparingly, mainly for news, football and hurling matches and a Saturday night programme on Radio Éireann called *Around the Fire*, which featured the singing of Seán Ó Síocháin, Martin Dempsey, Nellie Walsh, Joe Lynch and Art Sinnott, who was the best man ever to sing the rebel song 'Boolavogue'. My mother had a republican, anti-British streak in her and loved tuning in to Lord Haw-Haw, an Irish-American fascist politician and Nazi propaganda broadcaster whose real name was William Joyce. In his nightly news bulletins, he spread German propaganda and listed all the British casualties of the day. I know that at the time my mother was not aware of the awful and heinous war crimes of Hitler and the Nazi regime.

As well as tuning in to the radio, we also made our own entertainment, especially on dark winter nights. Maureen and I would settle ourselves, sitting snugly on my father's lap by the fireside listening to his many stories. He triggered our imagination with riveting tales about Celtic heroes, such as Cúchulainn, Fionn Mac Cumhaill and Oisín, and moved us to tears with stories about St Patrick being enslaved on Sliabh Mish. He sang to us too and had a huge range of Scottish songs, including a fishing song called 'Caller Herrin', 'Flora MacDonald' and 'I Belong to Glasgow'. He was a big fan of the songs of Harry Lauder. Most nights, he finished off with a stirring rebel song, such as 'The Boys of Kilmichael' or 'The West Awake'. Whenever my father sang, Maureen and I joined in too if we knew the words. When he sang a new song, we always picked up the chorus fairly quickly and learned the rest bit by bit.

My parents knew I had a good voice, which was a good boy soprano, pure and clear. Both of them encouraged me to sing and my father always warned me to watch out for when my voice would break, as it was important to stop singing while the new voice developed. But it all happened so gradually that I never even noticed the change.

In our house, we all loved singing and music so much that whenever a concert was held in Bantry, we always went along. One evening, when I was about eight years of age, we headed off to an open-air concert, known as Aeríocht, in the grounds of Bantry House. Among those taking part was probably the greatest *sean-nós* singer of all time, Cáit Ní Mhuineacháin

Seán, aged around six, at his father's former home in Adrigole, west Cork, with his favourite toy – with a bit of imagination, it could be anything.

from Ballingeary. During the interval, my father whisked me off to the courtyard of Bantry House and showed me the mangled wreckage of a German fighter plane that had crashed in nearby Kilcrohane. The sight and size of it filled me with awe. As we walked all around it, my father said that when the plane crashed a girl from Kilcrohane by the name of Shanahan came along and pulled out one of the Germans trapped inside. Some time later, she was invited to the German Embassy in Dublin and awarded the Iron Cross for her bravery. I was very impressed that we had such a heroine in the locality.

During the war, most local adult men joined one or other of the reserve forces in the Irish army, such as: the LDF, which was the local defence force and somewhat like today's FCA; the LSF, which was the local security force and aided An Garda Síochána; or An Slú Muirí, which was the naval reserve. All the forces carried out regular drills and manoeuvres around the area. One Sunday evening, I got the surprise of my life when eight LDF members took over our house and started a mock shooting with more LDF men who had planted themselves in the nearby woods and tried to capture our house.

But the biggest day of all was yet to come. On another Sunday, all the reserve forces joined together for a trooping of the colours ceremony in the square in Bantry. The atmosphere was electric and I nearly jumped out of my skin with excitement as I watched the forces proudly parade around the square, all in perfect step, to the rousing sound of a marching military band. Their uniforms impressed me too as all the troops were dressed to perfection, with their buttons and shoes gleaming and not a hair out of place. There was one exception though, my uncle Mort who was in the LSF. His beret was turned back to front and as he marched directly in front of me I shouted at him, 'Uncle Mort! Your cap is on back to front!' The faintest suggestion of a smile crossed his face. I went home on a high and made up my mind that I was definitely going to be a soldier when I grew up. Every day from then on, I put on a beret belonging to my father and marched around the house like a sergeant major, holding erect a sweeping brush with a yellow duster on top and singing 'Fáinne Geal an Lae' at the top of my voice.

But I had another uncle involved too. On Bere Island, my uncle Paddy O'Shea, who lived in Castletownbere, served as a civilian with the Irish army. Every night, when the army shone a huge search light over Bantry Bay, I thought of Uncle Paddy and took great pride in the fact that he was working with the military and I was sure he was the man in charge of the gigantic searchlight. Who else but my dear Uncle Paddy.

While the war continued, a hundred soldiers from the Second Cycling Squadron billeted in Bantry House. Sometimes, they came free-wheeling down the slope outside our house and made a funny swishing sound as they whizzed by.

On the first Friday of every month, which was a Fair Day in Bantry (when people traded their goods and animals), a recruitment officer from the British army came to the square. Later in the day, it was a common sight to see bicycles left abandoned at the railway station by local lads who had signed up with the British army.

One morning in 1946, as the war drew to a close, I was cycling to school with my father when one of the local gentry, Colonel Haskard, happened to come along on his bike. In a very superior tone of voice, he said to my father, 'O'Shea, we won the war.'

'Ye did indeed,' my father replied, and kept on cycling.

After the war, our lives changed rapidly. The rationing of food ended and my mother treated Maureen and me to our first banana and orange. Private cars took to the roads again and people began to travel more outside of their own locality.

Luckily for us, my father liked driving and drove us all over the place. Often, we'd head for high tea to the hotel in Gougane Barra owned by Dinny Cronin, who had been a classmate of my mother's and was known to all as Dinny Gougane. We'd no sooner be seated than Dinny would march into the dining room with a fag dangling from his mouth and say to my mother, 'Maggie, I've a nice bit of chicken for you,' as if he'd been keeping it all week especially for her. He was a loveable character and a rogue.

One of my favourite trips was going into Bantry every Saturday to do the shopping. As so few people had cars at the time, we were always able to park on exactly the same spot. Usually, Michael O'Leary, a teacher friend of my father's, sat into the car with him for a chat and a smoke while Maureen and I shopped with my mother. First we went to Swains' for knitting wool for Mam, then on to Biggs', a high-class grocery store. After my mother had finished her shopping, she treated us there to a four-penny jelly ice cream, which was an ice cream served in a glass with red, wobbly jelly on top. That was the highlight of our week. At some point, my father left the car also to do a bit of shopping too, as it was his job to buy the meat and some fish and bread.

Most Sunday evenings, we visited Uncle Mort and his wife Siobhán at Dad's home place in Adrigole. Many of the locals popped in while we were there. Usually, Maureen and I were the only children among the gathering, as Uncle Mort's children were away at secondary school. Most visits ended with a singsong. Everyone joined in. Some sang on their own too, among them my father, Uncle Mort and my aunts. Sometimes, my mother sang also, but only after much persuasion, as she found it hard to sing in front of people. She had a beautiful, sweet voice and one of her favourite songs was 'The Gypsy's Warning', the words of which advise a young girl not to trust her boyfriend. Whenever I was asked for a song, I usually sang 'Boolavogue', 'Seán Ó Duibhir' or *A Shaighdhiúirín a Chroí*'. More often than not, I sang from wherever I happened to be sitting, as did everyone else. An odd night, my mother would say, 'Stand out in the floor Seán and you'll sing better.' Sometimes, the adults played cards, with their favourite game being one hundred and ten. Most nights, we didn't leave to go home until after ten o'clock.

Each year on St Stephen's night, there was always a huge singsong. We looked forward to it almost as much as we did to Christmas itself and those annual singsongs are among my favourite childhood memories. My uncle Mort's family would be home on holiday for Christmas and they were all fine singers. In later years, Mort's son Con, who was a baritone, had his voice trained in Dublin. He studied all there was to learn about the human voice, as a result of which his technique was absolutely superb. He performed his songs in Irish, English, German and French. He was equally at home singing German *lieder* or Irish traditional. He sang regularly on Radio Éireann. His favourite song was a great ballad from the Famine era called 'The Union of Macroom'. In particular, I remember a rendition of it that he gave at a concert in Castletownbere. I hardly recognised him, as he appeared on stage dressed to kill in a white jacket, red bow tie and black trousers. I always admired him as a singer and a friend. When Con passed away some years ago, his widow Babs gave me his huge collection of songbooks. They are among my most treasured possessions.

Often on other family outings, we headed for the Beara Peninsula to watch a football match, as my father was a football addict, just like the rest of his family, and many of his nephews played the sport. On the way, we'd pick up Uncle Mort and his wife Siobhán. Maureen and I always toddled off with my father and Uncle Mort to watch the match, while my mother and Siobhán stayed chatting in the car. On the way back home, my father and Uncle Mort replayed every kick of the ball and usually gave the referee a fine roasting if their team lost.

In 1945, my father and his friend Christy O'Driscoll, a fellow teacher, went to Dublin by train for the All-Ireland senior football final between Cork and Cavan. It was a major event and they stayed in Dublin from Friday until Sunday. In the *Southern Star* the following week, the columnist Peadar Ó hAnnracháin gave a graphic description of a group of west Cork people parading up O'Connell Street: '… among them a former county footballer and schoolteacher in fine voice singing "The Banks of My Own Lovely Lee".'

Although no name appeared in the newspaper, somehow my mother seemed to know exactly the identity of the man in question. My father denied all charges.

In 1946, he went to the All-Ireland senior hurling champion-ship, in which Cork beat Kilkenny 7-5 to 3-8. He came home singing the praises of Christy Ring and replayed with passion

Christy's famous solo run of 50 yards, which ended with him banging the ball into the Kilkenny net. In the weeks to come, each time my father recalled it, the run got longer.

As well as bringing about changes in food and travel, the end of the war brought other changes too. The British general election of 1945 resulted in the defeat of the wartime leader and prime minister Winston Churchill. When he was replaced by the leader of the Labour party Clement Attlee, a lot of wealthy people expected his government to bring in a wealth tax. As a result, many rich English people and their families moved to Ireland. A lot of them settled in Ballylickey. Later, English tourists started to come to the village on holiday. At the time, Ballylickey had three good hotels: the Seaview; Ballylickey Manor House Hotel; and the Ouvane Hotel at Ballylickey Bridge. Farmers especially did well from the influx, as they were able to sell their food produce to the hotels. Over time, Ballylickey got a great name for its fresh, wholesome food.

Around that time too, a carpenter named Tim Manning bought a plot of land next door to us and built a carpenter's workshop there. Most days, I wandered into Tim and watched him busily at work at his trade. He was a nice, friendly man who usually found some job for me, in order to give me a sense of my own importance I think. Tim built a fine house next to ours and in due course he married a lovely lady named Joan Twomey, who hailed from Inchigeelagh. Joan had a good business sense and quickly spotted an opportunity for a shop. One day, when I called into Tim's workshop, the eyes nearly popped out of my head, as jars of barley sugar, bulls' eyes and liquorice allsorts stood before me, all neatly lined together on a shelf. Tim said, 'Joan is opening up a grocery shop and I'll be moving my workshop across the road. You'll have plenty of sweets on your doorstep then Seán.' Soon, the name Ó Mongáin appeared over the door and the grocery shop was up and running. It sold a wide range of fresh food products, all of which were in great demand by the English. Tim bought a small herd of Jersey cattle. Their milk had a high cream content, which was considered very nourishing in those pre-cholesterol times, and soon Joan began making her own ice cream. Her shop was the forerunner of Manning's Food Emporium, which stands on the same spot today and sells Irish artisan foods, cheeses, chutneys, honey and puddings and sausages of all shapes and sizes. It boasts a fine wine cellar too, with special emphasis on vineyards owned by families of Irish descent. For many years, the shop was run by Tim and Joan's son Val, one of my dearest and closest friends. He is the quintessential grocer and an expert on every kind of wine. He is a man of culture with wide and varying interests and a follower of every kind of sporting activity. I visit him as often as I can and I love to sit and chat to him outside his shop and catch up on the local lore. Most of all, I enjoy his impish sense of humour for he is a bit of a rogue. Recently, Val passed on the baton to the next generation of Mannings and he now divides his time between Ballylickey and his favourite Portuguese hideaway.

As well as the settlers and tourists, some famous people visited Bantry after the war. Many booked into Ballylickey

Seán, aged eight, and his sister Maureen, aged five, pose for a studio portrait at Leupold's, Cork. Seán's mother knitted the Fair Isle jumpers.

Manor House Hotel. At the time, the hotel was owned by the Graves family; indeed, it still is. They are descendants of the poet and balladeer Alfred Percival Graves, the man who wrote the famous ballad 'Father O'Flynn'. When the English foreign minister Herbert Morrison stayed at the hotel in the 1950s, the place was swarming with detectives, among them my best friend Eddie Bracken's father, Ned. One Saturday evening, Mr Bracken drove to our house in his brand new police car. I sat in to admire it and lo and behold he showed me his revolver. It was the first time I'd ever seen one. In 1948, Éamon de Valera booked into Ballylickey Manor House Hotel for three weeks to prepare for his world tour for the Anti-Partition League, which sought the reunification of Ireland by peaceful means. One evening, I was sitting by our gate when he strolled up the road. He spoke to me in Irish and was delighted that I was fluent in the language. Years later, when we met at a concert, I reminded him of our chat, but naturally enough he had no memory of meeting me.

After the war too, people began to enjoy all sorts of entertainment. In our house, going to the cinema on a Friday night became a tradition. I laughed my head off watching Laurel and Hardy films, *The Three Stooges* and *Old Mother Riley*, and I became a big fan of Bing Crosby after seeing him take the lead role in *Going My Way* and *The Bells of St Mary's*. We went to live shows in Bantry too, put on in the Old Town Hall or the Stella Cinema by travelling theatrical companies. We saw full-length plays such as *Othello*, *King Lear*, *Hamlet*, *Macbeth* and *Death of a Salesman,* all staged by the famous

Anew McMaster theatrical companies that toured the towns and villages of Ireland for nearly thirty-five years. McMaster was an extraordinary actor himself and his wife Marjorie, who was the sister of Micheál Mac Liammóir, also acted with the company. Later, many of the company's actors became internationally famous, among them, believe it or not, Harold Pinter. We enjoyed the fit-ups travelling variety shows also. Usually, they started with a variety show of singing, dancing and music, lasting about an hour. They followed that with a short version of a melodrama, like *Jane Eyre,* and ended with a funny sketch. Watching the performers on stage enthralled me, especially as I was still very shy. Sometimes, people who are shy take refuge in performing. Somewhere deep inside, they may have a burning desire to perform themselves and for me that yearning was awakened by the fit-ups. When I'd go to bed after seeing one of their shows, I'd dream about what the tenor had done on stage. I could almost visualise myself doing it.

But, talent wasn't confined only to the members of the touring companies, as we had much local talent too. In 1947, a world-renowned Irish traditional singer and piper, Séamus Ennis, drove into our yard in a black Ford Prefect to record my father and two other singers – the teacher and *sean-nós* singer Marcella Hurley and a wonderful, traditional, young singer named Mary O'Sullivan. Later, the BBC aired the recording on a radio show called *Turkey in the Straw.* Years afterwards, when I was recording at the BBC myself, I mentioned the 1947 recording to Brian George, a Donegal man, who was one of the top men there. Within minutes, he had dug out the recording and handed me a copy to keep of my father's soundtrack of a song called 'The Outlaw of the Hill'.

By 1949, it looked as if my enjoyment of all that Ballylickey and Bantry had to offer was about to come to an end, as I was due to start secondary school. At the time, Bantry had no secondary school for boys and my parents decided that I should try to become a boarder at Coláiste Íosagáin, which was run by the De La Salle order in the Gaeltacht, or Irish speaking, village of Ballyvourney, County Cork, and was located about 30 miles from home. My friend Eddie Bracken had already started there. By then, my notions of becoming a soldier had gone out the window and my parents assumed that I would follow in their footsteps and become a teacher. Along with other colleges, such as Coláiste na Mumhan in Mallow, Coláiste Íosagáin served as a preparatory college for teaching. But, I had one big hurdle to climb, as I had to do an entrance exam in Irish, English, maths, history, geography and singing, the test for which included an ear test and a sight test. With the help of my father I worked hard to prepare for the exam. It was held at Easter time in the convent school in Bantry. On the morning of the test, my father said to me, 'Bring home the test papers, Seán. Write down the answers you get to all your sums and I'll check to see if they're right.'

After sitting the exam, I was happy enough, even with the maths test, which had three hard sums and six easy ones. But, when my father checked my answers, he found that I hadn't got one single sum right. And so we decided that my chances of getting into Coláiste Íosagáin were nil.

Without wasting any time, my father made up his mind to uproot the whole family and move to Cork so that I could attend secondary school there. He applied for a job as a teaching assistant in the city and got it. During the summer months, he accepted the post and agreed to start the following August, even though he probably knew that he would be a total misfit in a city school.

Shortly after doing the exam, a cousin of mine named Seán O'Shea was due to be ordained as a priest. For the occasion, my father promised me my first long pants. But then, because I had failed my exam, he bought me a short one instead and a jacket to match.

In early August, I was kicking a football against the back of the house when my father appeared before me, beaming from ear to ear and waving a letter in his hand. 'Seán, you got Coláiste Íosagáin!' he said excitedly and threw his two arms around me. I said, 'I couldn't have.' He said, 'You did. You must have got the method of the sums right.' I could scarcely believe it. Indeed, it was the biggest surprise of my life and lifted a huge weight off my shoulders. And so my father never took up his new post in the city, where he was due to start in only a few weeks time.

On the following morning, he took me into Cullinane's shop in Bantry and said to Willie Cotter the draper, 'I want a suit for this man with long pants.' Willie stood back, looked at him in wonder and asked, 'But didn't you buy a suit for him some time ago?' Then, he said, 'There was a long pants going with it. I'll give you that.' And so I got my first long pants.

From then on, I was the centre of attention, with everyone congratulating me on my achievement, wishing me all the best for the future and my mother fussing over me, buying me a new pyjamas and suitcase and making sure that I had all my school books.

One Tuesday in early September, my parents came home early from school. I put my suitcase in my father's black Ford Prefect and all four of us headed for Coláiste Íosagáin.

As we drove on towards Ballyvourney, I was still delighted with myself and still on a high at having passed the exam. Yet, as we neared the college, I began to realise that I had no idea what lay ahead. Reality kicked in and all of a sudden I was filled with a terrible sense of apprehension.

2

COLÁISTE ÍOSAGÁIN

Although I had never before seen the college, I did have an idea about its location, as I had often been to nearby Inchamore, beside Coolea, to visit my mother's sister Nora who was married to a local farmer, Paddy Quill. But we always went by the scenic route through Béal a' Ghleanna and not through Ballyvourney.

As we drove through the big, iron gates of Coláiste Íosagáin, with its neat, colourful gardens at either side, I gazed up in awe at the tall, impressive, grey, stone building at the end of the avenue. How could I possibly settle in there? I had never before spent a night away from my family. I wondered what this new life would bring.

After saying goodbye to Maureen, who stayed in the car, I took my suitcase and walked into the college with my parents. We were shown to an office and introduced to the college president Brother Basil. He warmly welcomed us *as Gaeilge*, as it was an Irish-speaking college. At the time, the yearly fee for each student was £50, which could be paid in three instalments. My father parted with his money and bade goodbye to the brother and myself. As I watched my parents walk down the corridor, I felt sick with loneliness.

After being shown to my dormitory, I unpacked my suitcase and took time to take in my new surroundings. Built in 1936, the college still looked fairly modern, especially the dormitories, which were laid out with cubicles. That pleased me. At least I would have some bit of privacy. Yet, even though the building was relatively new, it felt damp. Later I learned that a fissure had opened between the outer ornamental stone cladding and the mass concrete wall, so much so that heavy rain was likely to leave pools of water on the floors of the cubicles. I quickly learned never to leave my socks or shoes on the floor.

As the day went on, more and more students came along and soon the dormitory was filled with noise and clatter. I realised that all of us were in the same boat, all starting a new life, away from home, in a strange place and not knowing what to expect. Still, that gave me no consolation whatsoever and my first night in the dormitory turned out to be one of the loneliest nights of my life.

On the following morning, the bell rang at half past seven. All the students gathered in the college chapel for Mass, which a young curate named Father Michael Twohig celebrated there every morning. In later years, I got to know him well. He was an extremely cultured man, a lover of music, and I frequently featured in his parish concerts.

After Mass, we went for breakfast to the refectory. Ten, long, rectangular tables lined the room. At one side, a brother sat at a table on a rostrum to supervise us. He said grace before and after the breakfast. On that first morning, talk was scarce enough amongst us newcomers. But gradually we struck up a conversation and soon got to know each other. We chatted away at break times between classes too and little by little I made friends with all my classmates. Over time, my loneliness faded away. Even to this day, I still keep in touch with some of the pals I made then.

In total, our class had eighteen students. Most of our teachers were brothers from the De La Salle order. While in the college, the brothers dressed in a long, black soutane with a big, white, starched collar. Outside, they wore a black suit and a full Roman collar with a thin black stripe down the centre to distinguish them from priests. They treated us well and rarely used corporal punishment of any kind. On the whole, they were decent, likeable men.

The president, Brother Basil, taught us catechism and led the rosary each night in the chapel. Every Thursday, he cycled to Macroom to play golf, a game at which he excelled. When he finished his game, he headed to the clubhouse for some liquid refreshment. We noticed that on the odd Thursday night, while saying the rosary, he sometimes mixed up the mysteries and sometimes too lost count of the 'Hail Marys'. We concluded it might have been the 'liquid refreshment', but sure the poor man had every right to a glass or two.

Brother Peadar – or An Bráthair Peadar as we called him – hailed from Valentia Island. We had barely set foot in the college when he enrolled the lot of us in the Pioneers, which meant that we made a promise not to drink alcohol ever, even if we lived to get the bounty from the president of Ireland. The pledge stood to me well in later life and I never broke it until I was in my late fifties.

An Bráthair Peadar taught English and Irish and was quite fanatical about the Irish language. I well remember that on the day King George VI died, he bounced into the classroom, hopped up on the rostrum, announced that he was giving us a free class, punched his fist in the air and shouted, '*Tá an Rí marbh!*', which means, 'The King is Dead!' Years later, I met him on a train to Dublin. He was on his way to visit a former pupil of his who had got a month in Mountjoy for selling Easter lilies.

A jovial Donegal man, Brother Anastasias taught maths and Irish. Although there wasn't an ounce of malice in him, he often gave us a rap around the knuckles with his key ring if we did something wrong. Brother George, a small, hyperactive man, was also a maths teacher, a really good one at that. Brother Bernadine from Wicklow was the football coach. He taught Latin, which I hated with a passion. The saving grace was that he could easily be diverted from the cursed Latin to discuss Gaelic football. As a result I got only 11 per cent in Latin in the Leaving Certificate, but I can keep my end up with any man or woman discussing the finer points of football.

We had three lay teachers. Ignatius Flanagan, a genial and popular Cork city man, taught us science. Murchadh Breathnach taught music and woodwork. In his music classes, he concentrated on giving us a large repertoire of songs, which we could use later as teachers. Even to this day, I still sing some of the songs he taught me, among them '*Iníon an Phailitínigh*' and '*Túirne Mháire*'. The most interesting of the three lay teachers was Dónal Ó Ciobháin from the Dingle Gaeltacht, who taught us history and geography. His method of teaching may not have been the best, as he took the easy option and simply read non-stop from his copious notes right through every class. But I found it a sheer joy to listen to the beautiful way he spoke Irish. Here was the Irish language in all its sweet glory. It was easy to agree with Thomas Davis' declaration, '*Tír gan teanga tír gan anam*' – 'A country without its language is a country without a soul' – when that language came from the mouth of Dónal Ó Ciobháin.

One of the most important people in the college was Miss O'Hanlon, our matron, whom students referred to as Mam. A nurse by profession, she looked after all our minor ailments and won the affection of each and every student.

When it came to learning, we were under no great pressure because passing the entrance exam to Coláiste Íosagáin had guaranteed us entry into St Patrick's College in Dublin, as long as we got honours Irish in our Leaving Certificate and a pass in certain other subjects, including music. At the time, St Patrick's was the only primary teacher training college in the republic for men and remained so until 1971.

On Saturdays and Sundays, we had no lectures and we had a half day every Wednesday. Usually, we strolled to Ballymakeera, just over a mile away. We visited Danny Jack Lucey's shop in the village, our unofficial tuck shop, where we parted with some of our pocket money. More often than not, I treated myself to a juicy slice of apple tart or a big, iced bun with a cherry on top and I washed it all down with my favourite drink – a pint glass of Ciderex, which tasted like Cidona but was served on draught from a barrel. Despite all my travels, I have never in my entire life come across Ciderex in any place other than in Danny Jack's.

If we weren't in the mood to trek all the way to Ballymakeera, we headed instead for Williams' shop, which was only a few hundred yards from the college, towards Killarney. It had a licensed public house at one end and a grocery section at the other. Today, it trades under the name The Mills Inn and is a popular pub, restaurant and music venue. Also, we gave some of our custom to Twohig's shop across the road, which was run by Mrs Twohig and her husband.

Sometimes, we did a bit of road bowling along the stretch of road between Ballyvourney and Coolea. It was there that I first met Seán Ó Duinín, who was known as An Gréasaí, which means the shoemaker. In later years, I got to know him well as a great *seanchaí* in the Fenian cycle tradition. Seán had a showband called the White Heather as well as a platform for open-air dancing between Macroom and Ballyvourney and many is the shilling I earned from him.

Now and again, local singers, storytellers and musicians came to the college to entertain us in the college hall. On one such night at Hallowe'en, a farmer named Dónal Ó Mulláin from Screathan near Coolea – who happened to be a next-door neighbour of my maternal grandfather Mike Twomey – gave a powerful rendition of one of his own compositions about a mad goat, 'An Poc ar Buile'. It blew me away, as it was a most unusual song, full of fun, with a lively, catchy chorus. I couldn't get the air out of my head and hummed it constantly for days afterwards. Little did I realise that the song would have such a huge impact on my life in time to come. Even now, I can still picture Dónal – a small, middle-aged man with a moustache – standing on the stage, belting out the song, with everyone joining in at the chorus. Many years later, I got to know his son Seán, who was a teacher in Passage East in Waterford. Dónal's daughter Joan, who also became a teacher, married a local man of great wit named Joe Kelly and Joan wrote a wonderful hymn in praise of St Gobnait, which was put to music by Peadar Ó Riada and is often sung at funerals and weddings in the church in Coolea.

Down through the years, the college had built up a great Gaelic football tradition, helped no doubt by the fact that most of its students came from Kerry, among them a contemporary of mine and one of Kerry's all-time greats, Tom Long from the Dingle Gaeltacht. The four famous Murphy brothers from Camp, Seán, Pádraig, Séamus and Tomás, who had a fistful of All-Ireland medals between them, lined out for the college too, as did Donal Hurley, a Barr's man from Cork city, who would also have pocketed a stack of All-Ireland medals had he been a Kerry man. Another fellow student and great pal of mine, Seán Higgins from Inchigeelagh, played with the Cork minor football team for three seasons in a row. In later years, his football career was greatly hampered by the fact that he spent all his teaching life in County Kilkenny, where he played with Kilkenny's junior football team until well into his fifties and almost single-handedly brought them to a Leinster junior football semi-final.

In Coláiste Íosagáin, the football teams competed very successfully in inter-college competitions organised by the Munster Colleges Council of the GAA. Indeed, during the four years I was there, they won the Munster Championship twice. Within the college, Brother Bernardine and Brother George organised inter-class competitions. Brother George picked two teams from the junior classes and they played a series of seven games against each other. Brother Bernardine used the same system with the two senior classes. On the day of the final match, the team with the highest cumulative score was declared the winner. That night, a special table was set aside in the refectory for the winning team and they received their award; a big pot of strawberry jam. Little physical training was done in those days, levels of fitness were not as high as they are today and players seldom moved beyond their own position on the pitch.

Although I tried with all my might to get on the football team, I failed miserably as I just didn't have the skill. Once, I won the hop, step and jump competition. That was my only sporting achievement at the college and was as low as a competitor could go in the field of sport. Nonetheless, I was always an ardent football supporter.

When our football team played, the entire college of eighty students went along to support them in what can only be described as an unusual mode of transport. At the time, a man in the village called Paddy Mick had a lorry with high creels for transporting turf. All eighty of us squeezed into Paddy Mick's lorry and headed for matches in places as far away as Cork city. We sang all the way, going and coming. On one such outing, during a heavy snow-fall, when we were on our way back from Millstreet, the creels broke and the senior students had to link arms for the whole journey to make sure the rest of us didn't fall off the lorry. Obviously, in those far off days, health and safety inspectors had not yet been invented.

All in all, food in the college was top-class and I took great pride in the fact that the cook Kitty Twomey was related to me. Young, local girls, including another cousin of mine, served our meals and we always glanced admiringly at them as they glided gracefully around the refectory with their trolleys. For breakfast, we usually had porridge, brown bread and boiled or scrambled eggs on weekdays, with a fry on Sundays. Lunch varied between fish, mutton and beef, with the tastiest dish of all being Kitty's legendary brown beef stew. We had a great selection of desserts too, apple tart galore, sherry trifle and bread and butter pudding, all beautifully presented by Kitty. Later when she married Pat Dineen and moved to Kilgarvan, Kitty built up a nice little earner for herself making wedding cakes and, together with Pat, opened a farm guest house called Hawthorn Farm. Many years later, when I had my own family, we went on holiday there year after year and ended up buying a tiny corner of a field from Pat where we put a mobile home. Over time, Kitty's little business went from strength to strength and she went on tours with Bord Fáilte to promote Ireland, with her signature dish being her brown scones.

While I loved the food in the college, I longed for a taste of my mother's home baking. Now and again, a parcel arrived in the post for me containing her homemade fruit cake, which was a big favourite of mine. Every single week without fail, my father wrote me a long letter. He filled me in on all the local and family news and gave me a full run-down on hurling and football matches.

Although I settled in well at the college and enjoyed my time there, I always looked forward to going home for the Christmas, Easter and summer holidays, especially as I saw my family only during the holidays. Once, when my father came to collect me, I was most impressed to see that he had bought a new Morris Minor, which was new on the market and was the most popular small family car at the time.

During the summer months at home, I spent most of my time swimming, going to football matches or cycling. I loved cycling and sometimes ventured as far as Adrigole to visit my Uncle Mort, a round trip of 40 miles. I went dancing to the Boys' Club Hall in Bantry and became a big fan of dance music. In those days, the bandsmen dressed in formal wear and sat behind their music-stands, reading and playing the various arrangements. The Boys' Club had been built almost entirely by a group of voluntary workers, led by the great Father (later Canon) James Horgan, who hopped into the trenches himself and helped dig out the foundations. Some years later, he played a huge role in building an even bigger dance hall at Gurranabraher in Cork city.

The Bantry Regatta was the main sporting and social event of the summer and always brought a great holiday atmosphere to the town. Indeed, many emigrants planned their holidays around the regatta. On the day, competitors and spectators poured into the town from far and wide. More than anything, I enjoyed watching the gig races between crews from Bantry, Bere Island, Castletownbere and Sneem. I had the pleasure of seeing the famous Casey brothers from Sneem compete, among them the eldest brother Steve, who had won the All-England Rowing Championship in 1936 with his brothers Paddy, Tom and Mick. For many years, Steve was the undisputed world champion professional wrestler based in the USA. In size, the brothers were massive. Their father was big Mick Casey, a bare-knuckle boxer who had sparred in his youth with John L. Sullivan, while their mother Brigid Sullivan hailed from a family around Sneem known as 'The Mountains'. Today, a statue of Steve Casey stands proudly in Sneem, a well-deserved tribute to a unique man.

Apart from running rowing competitions, the regatta held other contests too, such as 'The Greasy Pole'. Competitors had to walk the full length of the pole, clutch the flag on the end and make their way back to the starting point. Whenever anyone lost their balance and plunged into the sea, the crowd left out an almighty roar. That competitor was then eliminated. The final person standing was declared the winner.

During the summer holidays of 1953, I made my first ever trip to Dublin, along with the whole family, in the Morris Minor. From the time we set out from Ballylickey, my father was a bag of nerves, as he had never before driven to Dublin and felt totally out of his depth. He was in mortal dread of contraptions installed at junctions in Dublin called 'traffic lights'. But he got us there eventually and we headed to Croke Park to watch Galway take on Kilkenny in the All-Ireland hurling semi-final, which was the highlight of our weekend. Looking back, I think the whole purpose of the trip may have been to give me a taste of Dublin, as the time was drawing near for me to start at St Patrick's College, provided, of course, that I got the necessary marks in my Leaving Certificate. Thankfully, it all worked out in my favour.

While I had enjoyed my years at Coláiste Íosagáin, when it came to leaving, I had mixed emotions. At the end of the day, especially for a young man of my age, Dublin was a huge attraction.

3

St Pat's

I was not the first member of my family to study at St Patrick's Training College in Drumcondra, or St Pat's as it was commonly known. In the early years of the twentieth century, my uncles Seán and Mort attended there to become national teachers. In those days, students were served a bottle of Guinness at breakfast. The authorities were not as tolerant in my day and alcohol was strictly forbidden. Indeed, during my time there two students came to grief. One was caught by the dean as he returned to the college with some Guinness on board following a night out. He was gone next morning. The second, a Connemara man, brought back some poteen after the Christmas. He decided to have a drop in the dormitory late one night and, fortified by the good old mountain dew, broke into a verse of a *sean-nós* song. He too got a straight red card from the dean.

I arrived in St Pat's in September 1953 to begin the two-year training course. In all, the college had about three

Seán is pictured second on the left in the front row in June 1955 for his graduation from St Patrick's Training College, Dublin.

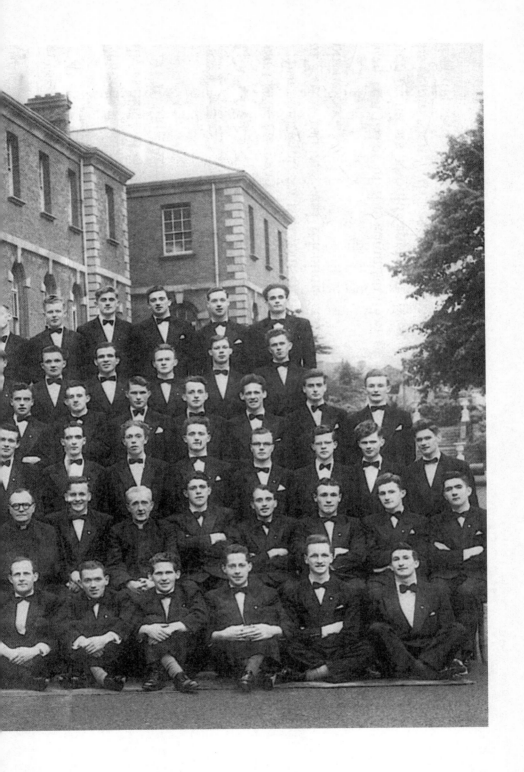

hundred students. The 150 or so first-year students were known as 'Hedgers', while those in second year were known as 'Gents'. Like Coláiste Íosagáin, the dormitories were laid out in cubicles, although they were not as modern. So too, meals at St Pat's were not on par with those served at Coláiste Íosagáin.

The curriculum of the two-year course at St Pat's included the study of education and teaching methods, as well as the practical experience of teaching for two weeks each year in St Patrick's National School, which was located in the grounds of the college. Its most famous past pupil is the former *taoiseach* Bertie Ahern.

Our professor of education was a wonderful man named Michael Jordan, father of Neil, the internationally acclaimed film director and fiction writer. Totally dedicated to his profession, Professor Jordan was extremely practical in relating the theory and practice of teaching to us and I hope Neil knows that his father was such a fine educationalist.

All subjects were taught through English and this caused huge problems for former students of Coláiste Íosagáin, especially in the study of maths. Now, we had to grasp an entirely new vocabulary, with many technical terms. I found it almost impossible to get to grips with them and never really got into my stride with the maths class.

For music, we had a great teacher named Seán Hayes from High Street in Cork. I auditioned to join his superb choir but he turned me down, without giving any reason. Naturally, I was taken aback by his decision. But, in later years, when we happened to bump into each other, Seán explained that he had rejected me simply because my voice was too distinctive for a choir. And he was right. Both of us had a good old laugh about it.

Without a doubt, the biggest difference between Coláiste Íosagáin and St Pat's was the social life. Since my days in Ballyvourney, I had two great pals, Vincent Hanley from Eyeries and Seán Higgins from Inchigeelagh. Bernie O'Sullivan from Cahermore in Beara, who arrived from St Brendan's College Killarney, teamed up with our gang and the four of us made the most of our time in Dublin.

On Sunday nights, we could stay out until eleven o'clock and dancing became a big pastime. Most Sunday nights, we headed to a student dance in Conarchy's Hotel in Parnell Square. Once a month, we made our way to the Crystal Ballroom in Anne Street South for an afternoon dance with the girls from Carysfort College in Blackrock, which trained Catholic girls for teaching.

In those days, no dance hall was licensed to sell alcoholic drink. All the girls lined up on one side of the hall and all the men on the other. When the band announced a dance, the males rushed to the other side to ask the girls out to dance. At the time, I still had a boyish look about me and could quite easily be mistaken for a primary school pupil rather than a trainee teacher. So any self-respecting girl might not relish the idea of me approaching her. To avoid a refusal, I'd dash across the floor at an angle of 45 degrees and do a quick change of direction so that I'd be standing right in front of the girl ever before she got a chance to have a good look at me. In those times, it was considered rude to refuse anyone to dance and so, luckily for me, I was never short of partners. After three dances, if you liked your partner a lot, you might ask her to stay on for the next set of dances and maybe later invite her to the mineral bar. Indeed it used to be said in west Cork that many a woman lost a fine farm of land simply because she wasn't thirsty enough at the right time.

Sometimes, romances blossomed and faded, although I do know of a few fellow students who met their future wives in Conarchy's Hotel. But, back then, romance was a gradual affair, unlike in today's world, where I am told a relationship can start at a disco on a Sunday night, be really serious by Monday and end with a text on Tuesday.

As well as going dancing, we spent many nights at the cinema. We sat glued to the screen as we watched Hitchcock's gripping thrillers *Rear Window* and *Dial M for Murder*, both of which starred Grace Kelly, who we decided was the most beautiful woman we had ever seen. We loved British comedies too and laughed our heads off at *The Belles of St Trinian's*, *Doctor in the House* and *Happy Ever After*, which featured David Niven. The film I remember best and liked most of all was Bill Haley's *Rock Around the Clock*. That film, I think, gave birth to rock and roll and modern-day pop music.

Croke Park became another favourite venue. One particular hurling match between Wexford and Clare, in a now defunct competition called the Oireachtas Cup, stands out in my mind. Around that time too, Bishop Lucey was building his rosary of churches in Cork and a fundraiser challenge match in Croke Park was arranged between St Vincent's Hurling Club from Dublin and Glen Rovers from Cork. St Vincent's had a powerful hurler named Norman Allen and of course the Glen had the mighty Christy Ring. The match drew a huge crowd and, in the clash of the ash between Allen and Ring, there was only one clear winner; the bould Christy himself. That day, I saw Christy do something that I never saw anyone do since. From a puck-out, he didn't double on the ball, but he stopped it for a moment on the *bas* of his hurley and then he pelted it over the bar. A poem about Christy by the great Cork poet Seán Ó Tuama springs to mind. To paraphrase it, he said that every Sunday we go to the park to see Christy play in the hope that he might do something supernatural and sometimes he achieves this. For me, that day in Croke Park was one such day.

Like all third-level colleges in Ireland at the time, St Pat's boasted its own battalion of the FCA, the army reserve, and I became one of its most enthusiastic members. Every Sunday morning, we carried out a drill dressed in our full uniform and armed with unloaded rifles. On St Patrick's Day, we marched around Drumcondra, all in perfect step, with our heads held high. We felt extremely proud of ourselves and of our uniform. One Sunday morning, we headed off to the Gormanstown army rifle range in County Meath, where each of us got the chance to fire six shots at a target board. At the time, I was a rather puny teenager and each kick from my rifle destabilised me to such an extent that, far from getting a bull's-eye, none of my shots even hit the target board. However, my friend Vincent

Hanley, who was standing on my left, ended up with seven bullet holes on his board, which meant that one of my shots must have strayed over to him. While our outings were always enjoyable, for me, the best perk of being an FCA member was the uniform's heavy overcoat, which came in especially handy to throw on the bed on cold winter nights.

At the end of the first year, I was sent to sixth class in St Patrick's National School for my first two-week teaching practice. The class was taught by a man named Kevin O'Shea from Glengarriff, who happened to be related to me through marriage. At about half past ten on my first morning there, as I was teaching a lesson in Irish, Kevin was called outside. When he came back minutes later, he told me that his father, Pádraig Ó Séaghdha, a well-known Irish scholar and poet, had died suddenly in Glengarriff. As well as being the author of some books, Pádraig had also written many Irish pamphlets, using his *nom de plume* Gruagach an Tobair. At the time of his death, he was in his nineties. After telling me the sad news, Kevin gave me a pat on the shoulder and said, 'Seán, you'll be on your own for the rest of the week.' This was a big challenge, but the many times I played school with my sister Maureen gave me a weird kind of experience which I put to good use and I was quite happy with myself that I managed the week's teaching on my own without any great problem. Also I'm sure the fact that teaching was in my blood helped. Indeed I never considered any other way of life except teaching.

My second year at St Pat's was every bit as enjoyable as the first and seemed to pass by in the blink of an eye. All too soon, it was time to carry out our final teaching practice, for which we would be graded from A to D. The grades themselves had no bearing on our levels of pay, yet the higher the grade the better the job prospects. At the end of the two years we had to sit the final examination on which our careers depended and which was known as the Senior Final. All lectures finished a month before the examination. This meant that we had four weeks to study. In my case, I had to make up feverishly for all the time I had spent dancing, going to the cinema, attending matches and parading around with the FCA. Thankfully, the examination went off without any great hitch.

The final event of our sojourn in St Pat's was the graduation dance in Cleary's Ballroom, situated in the top floor of the famed department store in O'Connell Street. It was a posh affair, formal dress and all that. Each of us had to find a partner, which posed no problem for any of us who had girlfriends. Some weeks before the ball, those of us without partners went along to the Crystal Ballroom in the hope of meeting some girls from Carysfort College who were in the same plight as ourselves. Towards the end of the night, I struck gold with a pretty girl from the west of Ireland. She proved to be the ideal partner and we had a wonderful night together at the graduation dance. I never again set eyes on her. I hope she had a happy life and that she is still hail and hearty. After the dance, as the dawn was breaking, my friends and I walked back to St Pat's Training College for the last time.

When I woke after a few hours' sleep, it suddenly dawned on me that my days as a student were well and truly over. I was now a teacher like my father and mother, five uncles and aunts and countless cousins. I enjoyed my days in Pat's and the friendships I made there still endure, except where the Grim Reaper has intervened. May those who have gone rest in peace.

Having qualified as a teacher, it was time to move on once again and to begin yet another new phase in my life.

4

BALTINGLASS

As I had loved Dublin so much, I wanted to find a teaching post in a school not too far away so that I could go back to the city for a weekend every now and then. And so, when I spotted an advertisement for an assistant teacher in the boys' national school in Baltinglass, County Wicklow, I immediately applied.

On 1 July 1955, at the age of nineteen, I hopped on the bus and made my way to Baltinglass in southwest Wicklow for an interview with the parish priest Father Tom Gahan. Much to my surprise, Father Tom asked me only one question, 'Can you play the organ for Benediction my young man?'

'I can indeed Father,' I replied, even though at the time I could barely master a few chords of '*O Salutaris*'. Without further ado, he shook my hand and said, 'The job is yours.' Funnily enough, during all my time in Baltinglass, nobody ever asked me, not even once, to play the organ.

When I moved to Baltinglass, the town was still feeling the effects of the Battle of Baltinglass, which was a local rumpus caused about the appointment of a sub-postmaster. Seemingly, the family who had held the post office for a long time had lost it because of political intervention. As well as being the talk of the town, the furore drew the attention of both the local and the international media.

From the day I started as a teacher in the school, I found all the staff pleasant, kind and helpful to the newly-arrived recruit and the principal R. L. Barron was especially good to me. My classroom itself was not the best. Known as 'the gallery', it had rows of steps and no desks. The children sat on the steps and wrote with their copybooks on their laps. For about thirty minutes each day, the principal gave my class the use of his room so that the children could practice their writing.

During my time in Baltinglass, I lived in lodgings across the road from the school owned by a widow named Nellie Byrne, whose late husband I had succeeded in the school. A chain smoker who liked a little tipple now and again, Nellie was a wonderful cook and a generous woman also. She kept two other male lodgers, a banker and an ESB worker, as well as a young teacher from Clare named Mary McMahon, who became a great friend of mine. Shockingly, a few years ago, Mary and her husband were murdered in a horrific family tragedy. I felt numb for days after hearing of their deaths.

For a small, rural town, the social life in Baltinglass was good, with plenty of sporting activities and facilities, such as a football club, tennis courts, badminton, an open-air swimming pool – as the River Slaney ran through the town – and a golf course. People from all walks of life joined the golf club, which was unusual in Ireland in the 1950s when golf was played almost exclusively by the well-to-do.

Every Sunday night, the golf club ran a dance. On one particular night, a local band called The Blue Moon Showband needed a piano player and asked me to sit in for the gig. My piano skills were limited, much like my organ playing, as I had taken piano lessons for only a short time when I was a child. But, I gave it my best shot and now hold the dubious distinction of having played the piano with a dance band while really not being able to play the piano at all.

As my first term in Baltinglass came to an end, I prepared to head home to Ballylickey for the holidays, full of Christmas cheer and totally unaware that our loving, close-knit family was about to be hit by a terrible tragedy.

5

A TIME OF SORROW

Is é an cladhaire an bás a thagann
Go ciúin gan caint na teangan
Ar nós an taoide leathan
I gcuantaibh do shaol

Death is a robber that comes
Quietly without speech of tongue
Like the wide tide
In the harbours of your life

Christmas 1955 was meant to be the best Christmas ever.
How could it be other than that? At last I was a teacher;
my childhood dream had become a reality. I had my own few
shillings in my pocket and had great plans to spend them all
over Christmas.

We got our holidays in Baltinglass on the Friday before
Christmas. That evening, I headed for Dublin and danced
the night away in the Television Club in Harcourt Street. On

the following day, I took an early train to Cork. The citizens of the second city were in a state of shock as their beloved Opera House had been completely destroyed by fire the night before. I continued by bus to Bantry, where my parents were waiting for me, along with my sister Maureen, who was home from Drishane convent school, where she was a boarder. We completed the journey to Ballylickey by Morris Minor.

On Christmas morning, we rose at dawn to go to the first three Masses in Bantry, as was the custom at the time. The first Mass started at eight o'clock and the same priest said each Mass, one after the other. After the last Mass, as we came through the door of the church, there was a sudden crush. Once outside, my father complained of a bit of a pain in his chest. We took no notice. We had a most enjoyable and traditional Christmas Day, turkey with loads of potato stuffing, followed by my mother's plum pudding, made from a recipe she claimed had been in her family for generations.

But, later that night, while I was listening to the Chris Lamb Big Band on Radio Éireann, my father got irritated with me for having the radio too loud. We had a few words about it and relations between us were still a little strained when we went to bed.

On the next morning, St Stephen's Day, I went out to the garage, where my father was chopping sticks for the fire. I apologised for what had happened the night before. He readily accepted and we were friends again.

Some time later, when I was back in the house, I heard a knock on the front door. I thought it might be the wren boys, as the St Stephen's Day tradition of children or adults going from door to door, dressed in costume, singing and collecting money, was still strong in our area. I was wrong. It was my father. The minute I opened the door, he rushed past me without saying a word and ran up the stairs. For some strange reason, a few minutes later, I followed him. When I walked into his bedroom, I saw him half sitting on the bed, with one leg hanging out over the edge and a big tear rolling down his left cheek. He was dead.

The man who was never sick in all his life was gone in a flash and, also in a flash, grief, sorrow, sadness and desolation engulfed me. I stared at him in desperation, hoping I was wrong, hoping for some sign of life, some blinking of an eye, maybe a smile for me, even if it was to be the last one. Bizarrely, the thought struck me that the man who was never sick a day was also the man who smoked sixty, maybe seventy, Sweet Afton every day, most of them late at night as he completed his crossword puzzles.

I roared for my mother and Maureen. They came up straight away. I will never forget their sobs and their wails. My mother had lost a kind, devoted and loving husband. Maureen and I had lost a kind, generous and loving father. Our lives were changed, utterly changed. By nature, Maureen is a calm person. But she cried non-stop. In Irish, there is a phrase called, '*In iomar na h-aimiléise*', which means, 'In the trough of sorrow'. That's where we were at around half past two on St Stephen's Day 1955.

Very quickly, we came to our senses. I ran about a quarter of a mile to our nearest neighbours, the Manning family, who had a phone. In no time at all, the local curate Father Dan Joe McCarthy, a genial and saintly priest, came and anointed my father. I asked Father McCarthy if the anointing had been done in time, as my father had already passed away when he arrived. He assured me that he had been in plenty of time and told me that the soul takes quite a while to leave the body. Our local doctor Jerry Murphy came quickly too. He could do very little apart from confirming that my father was dead. Garda Superintendent O'Donovan and Donal Creedon, the local coroner, also arrived. Without any fuss, they satisfied themselves that my father had died a natural death. When somebody dies suddenly, all of these procedures must be carried out and rightly so.

As quickly as we could, we got word by telephone to our close family relations. My uncle Mort was the first to come. He was indeed a broken man. I always knew that my father and himself were close and his pain that day proved it.

Later that evening, our local postman Eddie Wiseman was the first to call to sympathise with us and share our sorrow. Over the next few days, a constant stream of people came to the house. Each and every person who called lightened our burden somewhat and lifted us a little bit by sharing their grief with us.

My father had always been a friendly, humble, ordinary man and a popular one too. His sudden passing brought tears to the eyes of many who came, among them his past pupils, all our neighbours, his friends from the teaching profession and from the sporting world, as well as relatives from far and near.

Around six o'clock on the evening of 27 December, my father was placed in his coffin. My mother, Maureen and I, along with a few family members, including Uncle Mort, said a final farewell to him before the coffin lid was closed.

As the coffin was brought down the narrow stairs, it chipped a little of the banister, about halfway down. Afterwards, every time I went up and down the stairs, that notch reminded me of the terrible trauma of St Stephen's Day.

My mother wanted to bury my father in the cemetery beside the parish church in Bantry. But we were told that the graveyard was full and that no more plots were available. At that time, a man called Jackie the Canon worked for the parish priest. He looked after the church and the graveyard and carried out small repairs to the schools of the parish. When Jackie heard of my mother's plight, he sent word to her that there were three vacant plots at the corner of the cemetery, near the church. The parish priest agreed that my mother could have them on condition that she bought all three graves.

I have little recollection of the funeral Mass or of the burial ceremony, as I was totally overwhelmed and bowed down by all that was taking place around me. On that awful day, only one thought filled my mind; my father whom I had loved and adored was gone from our lives forever.

That night, and for several nights after, as I lay in my bed, trying to get to sleep, I would think of him, cycling beside me to school, talking with passion about football and, most of all, singing songs by the fireside and all the songs he taught me. In my heart, I knew our home would never be the same again.

6

Warner's Lane

The journey back to Baltinglass to resume teaching after my father's passing was sad and lonely, a total contrast to the joyful one in the opposite direction a few weeks earlier. Every mile of the way, I was thinking of him, the times we had together, the matches he took me to, the songs he taught me, all the advice he gave me, the problems I brought to him that he usually solved, the wisdom he tried to instil in me and the care he took to teach me the 'facts of life'. Then there were the 'what ifs?' What if we had insisted he went to the doctor when he complained of the chest pain on Christmas morning? And I cursed the Sweet Afton cigarettes. I worried about my mother and my sister and how they would cope with the loss.

Life in Baltinglass was difficult too. It was the custom of the time to observe a strict period of mourning for twelve months following the death of a parent. It meant giving up entertainment, such as the cinema, dancing and concerts. As a result, I saw less and less of my friends. We drifted apart somewhat. To signify the mourning, it was normal to wear a black tie and a black diamond on the jacket sleeve. Although I never really got over the sudden death of my father, I tried my best to get on with life.

Shortly before my father passed away, he had started teaching me how to drive his new Morris Minor. About a week after his burial, sure that I had fully mastered the skills required, I took to the road and began driving my mother in and out of Bantry to do her shopping. One evening, as I was driving her home, I turned swiftly into our avenue only to find that somebody had closed the gate. I drove right through it. My mother was not at all impressed and told me exactly what she thought of my driving. Although she never learned to drive, she was a powerful navigator and had never allowed my father exceed 30 miles per hour. In her absence, he was quite a nifty driver.

Every week in Baltinglass, I wrote to my mother. Each time she replied, I could see that she was very down indeed. When I went home for the Easter holidays, we decided that I should try for a teaching post nearer to home. Luckily, when I applied for a vacancy as an assistant teacher at St Patrick's Boys' National School in Bandon, I got the job.

Known locally as Warner's Lane, the school had a great principal, a local man named Liam Ó Donnchadha. Indeed I learned more in a year from Liam about the practicalities of teaching than I had learned in my two years at St Pat's training college. Liam was a strict disciplinarian but he tempered his strictness by showing kindness and friendship to all his pupils, especially to those he might have punished for some reason or other. For instance, if Liam disciplined a boy early in the morning, he made sure to single out that boy for special attention later and would pass every ball to him in a puck-around in the playground during the eleven o'clock break. Liam came from a strong republican background and tragically one of his brothers was shot dead in Bandon during the War of Independence, or the Troubles as it was called. A great historian, Liam knew all there was to know about his native town and its environs. He was a fluent Irish speaker and was chairman of the local branch of the Gaelic League, an organisation founded in 1893 by Douglas Hyde – who subsequently became the first president of Ireland – to revive the Irish language.

On top of all of that, Liam was hugely passionate about hurling, especially Bandon hurling, and he trained the school team. During my first year in Bandon, the pupils from the boys' national school in nearby Clonakilty beat the boys from Warner's Lane by about twenty-three goals. Such a rout is always highly possible in schoolboy games. As Liam and I walked off the pitch together, he assured me through gritted teeth that this would never happen again. He kept his word. For the next fourteen years, with Liam still holding the reins, Warner's Lane won the West Cork Schoolboys' Championship, often by scores even greater than twenty-three goals.

At Liam's suggestion, I joined the Gaelic League. I was happy to do so and then he more or less appointed me secretary. The branch organised music nights, concerts, *céilís* and lectures and I got to talk a lot of Irish, which I was very happy about. I

Bantry Blues won the Cork County Championship (football) for the first time in September 1995 and a proud Seán Ó Sé joined the victorious team to sing 'Bantry Bay'.

also tried my best to play football with Bandon, but without success. Yet, somehow or other, I ended up with a West Cork Junior B Championship medal. There was little or no prestige attached to that medal. Any self respecting footballer might not even bother to bring it home with him. But me, I have it still and I value it. I suppose it proves that I at least tried to play the game. I remember one particular match when I got a signal from a mentor, a good friend of mine, to lie down so that I could be replaced. When I reached the sideline, his comment said it all, 'Jesus, Lizzie would do better.' Lizzie was the parish priest's housekeeper and close to pension age.

July 1958. Seán (*on right*) holidaying in Ballybunion with friends (*l–r*)
Munchin O'Connell, Bernard McGuinness and Liam Cantwell RIP.

My best friend in Bandon was a Kinsale man named
Munchin O'Connell, whom I met at Nellie O'Mahony's
house in Oliver Plunkett Street in Bandon, where we both had
lodgings. At the time, Munchin was working as a postman.
Later, he became a customs official. Unlike me, he was a very
handy footballer and also played with Bandon. Nobody ever
compared him to Lizzie. He was a good wingback and an
excellent goalkeeper. Indeed, he played in goal for the Cork

senior team. To this day, he remains my closest friend. Every week, we meet up for coffee and often recall our exploits in Bandon.

Back then, the showband era had well and truly arrived and the Lilac Ballroom in Enniskeane was in its heyday. My mother gave me possession of the Morris Minor and every Sunday night a car-load of us headed for the Lilac Ballroom and danced the night away to bands such as the Clipper Carlton which was my own favourite, Brendan Boyer and the Royal Showband, Butch Moore and the Capitol Showband and Cork's famous Brendan O'Brien and The Dixies.

While teaching in Bandon, my mother suggested that I should continue my education and go to UCC by night. But the idea didn't appeal to me. Anyway, I had failed Latin in my Leaving Certificate, which meant that I would have to sit the matriculation exam to gain entry to university. Besides, I had no desire whatsoever to take up the books again.

As it happened, one night while I was strolling along in the city, I saw a notice flyer on a window of the Cork School of Music advertising singing lessons. I figured that these lessons might pacify my mother. I walked straight in and was auditioned on the spot by a man named John T. Horne. A highly respected choir-master, teacher and musician, he was known as Jock to his friends, but not so to any of his pupils: to them he was always Mr Horne. He came from a well-known Cork city family and he still holds the distinction of directing and conducting the Cork School of Music choir when they won the International Trophy at the Cork Choral Festival, the only Irish choir ever to do so. As well as conducting the choir and giving singing lessons, John T. Horne was the resident organist at St Finbarr's Cathedral in Cork. For my audition, he asked me to sing a few scales and made up his mind there and then to take me on.

On the following Tuesday evening at five o'clock, I started my first ever singing lesson with him. Before we began, he pondered for a moment, as he was unsure whether he should train me as a baritone or a tenor. Then, as if he had been inspired, he said with great enthusiasm, 'I'll take you up a few tones and make you a tenor.' About ten minutes into the half-hour lesson, he suddenly stopped and asked me if I was a smoker. At that time, if I was out socialising, I sometimes inhaled the very odd Consulate. These menthol cigarettes came with the catchy blurb, 'Cool, clear Consulate – as clear as a mountain stream.' When I admitted my indulgence, John T. Horne banged down the lid of the piano and warned me not to come back the following week unless I had given up the cigarettes.

From the time I started the singing lessons, my voice improved. John T. Horne worked on the voice and the breathing, knocked off the rough edges and greatly extended my range. He was a wonderful teacher of vocal technique mainly because, while he developed the voice, he left it its individuality, its natural qualities and distinctiveness. In those days, it was par for the course for many singing teachers to try and change their male pupils into the latest version of John McCormack. I have always been conscious of the fact that a good voice is a gift from God and John T. Horne told me in the early days of tutoring me that the Good Lord had also granted me good breathing, which meant I had to do very few breathing exercises.

Four years later, during my last lesson with him, he advised me that if I did not abuse my voice it would last practically as long as my body. Today, at almost eighty years of age, I can say so far so good. I am quite certain that my singing career would have ended many years ago but for John T. Horne.

Meanwhile, as well as improving my singing, other changes were afoot, I said a fond farewell to Warner's Lane and Bandon itself and took up a new teaching post in Cork city. By then, my mother had already moved to the city and my sister Maureen had been teaching there for some time.

My new posting was the Cathedral Boys' School in Cathedral Road, Gurranabraher. This school was built in the 1930s to cater for the children of the newly-built suburb of Gurranabraher. The school was known as The New School and even though many other schools were later built in the area and it is no longer a school, the building is still referred to as The New School.

And so I began yet another new and challenging part of my career, in an area known as The Red City. It got its nickname not because of any political leanings of its residents but because all the houses had red tiled-roofs.

7

The Red City

In 1962, I arrived at the Cathedral school. In fact, by the time I got there, the school had passed its peak and was in what eventually proved to be its terminal decline. At one time, over six hundred scholars attended this ten-classroom school. This was an average of sixty pupils per classroom. Talk about sardines in a tin! How the teachers and, indeed, the pupils coped I will never understand. But cope they did. In its glory days, the school's standards were reputed to be well above the average. Falling enrolment saps the morale and it was low in the Cathedral school by the time I got there. The other four teachers and I found teaching there a constant struggle. Yet, it had its benefits too and gave me the chance to get to know the great people of the northside of Cork city. They liked to refer to themselves as 'Norries'. I did not foresee it at the time but I was to spend the rest of my teaching career among the Norries, some thirty-one years, in fact.

In all my time among them, I found that they were the finest people one could meet. They were friendly, honest in their dealings and never held a grudge. Most of them were blessed with a keen sense of humour, the style of which was uniquely their own. Also, they had a great love of singing and had a huge repertoire of their own songs, such as 'The Boys of Fairhill' and 'The Armoured Car'.

They were famous too for their love of opera, especially operatic choruses, a taste for which they may have developed at the nearby Cork Opera House, across the River Lee, where many touring English operatic companies often performed in former times.

As well as their great love of music in general, northsiders had a huge *grá* for all types of sport. They had their harrier clubs, their pigeon lofts and of course Glen Rovers in Blackpool, the most famous hurling club in Cork, where the legendary Christy Ring and the famous Jack Lynch displayed their wares. And they played the almost exclusively Cork game of road bowling, mostly in the boreens around the northside. Their most famous bowl player was Timmy Delaney, whom I had the privilege of meeting a few times. In the famous ballad 'The Boys of Fairhill', which was composed by the northside poet and songwriter Seán O'Callaghan, bowl playing gets a verse all to itself:

'Come on boys and spend a day with our bowl players so gay
The loft of the bowl it would make your heart thrill
When you hear the Shea boys say, "Timmy Delaney won today"
Evergreen bows to the boys of Fairhill.'

Interestingly, the Shea boys mentioned in the song came from a famous family of bowl players. One of my closest friends is the renowned northside singer John O'Shea, also known as 'The Singing Fireman' and he is a proud member of that clan. A handy bowl player himself, he is still throwing away at over eighty years of age. He has many fine qualities, but most of all he is a genuine Shea boy.

Another northside passion was hunting. Most northside men had either a hunting dog or a terrier and most of them too were affiliated to one of the harrier clubs in the area. Some were pigeon fanciers and many back gardens had pigeon lofts. Sometimes, the racing pigeons were transported to England and they raced back to Cork where their owners anxiously awaited their return to their lofts.

While I taught at the Cathedral school, I nearly always had the senior classes and so the big task of the school year was preparing for the sacrament of Confirmation. The most important event of any Confirmation year, apart from the day of the Confirmation itself, was the day the bishop came to examine the boys in their religious knowledge.

At the time, Dr Cornelius Lucey, the bishop of Cork and Ross, was one of the most high profile bishops among the Irish hierarchy. He was known for his outspoken sermons on social matters, preached usually at Confirmations, and he was one of the first persons ever to speak out bravely about the neglect of rural Ireland, and in particular west Cork, which he always pointed out was being unfairly treated by the government of the day.

As a Confirmation examiner, he was serious, strict and thorough. However, I always noticed that if a boy fared poorly in the Confirmation examination, Dr Lucey would have a word in the teacher's ear to enquire about the boy's circumstances. If he was satisfied that the boy had made an honest effort to pass the exam, he left him through. On the other hand, if the boy had made no attempt at all to prepare for the test, the bishop would tell him that he would have to wait another two years before being confirmed and he would advise him to go off and learn his catechism in the meantime.

While I was in the Cathedral school, a young teacher named Tom O'Herlihy joined the staff. He arrived straight from St Pat's and very quickly we became firm friends. He is a native of Kilnamartyra, a lovely village situated halfway between Macroom and Ballyvourney. He was not long with us when he married the love of his life, Nancy Troy from County Tipperary. Nancy is a well-known Irish dancing teacher and a much sought-after adjudicator. Tom is a handy friend to know, as the saying goes he is very good with his hands, and in addition he is very generous with his time.

In parallel with my teaching, the singing was moving along nicely. I liked teaching but when the school day was finished it was great to have something different to turn my attention to. And indeed maybe they are not all that different, teaching and singing, as both have an element of performance in them.

8

THE SINGER

Back in November 1959, my cousin and good friend Kathleen O'Shea entered me for the traditional singing competition in Feis na Mumhan and even paid the fee to make sure I would turn up. She knew I had no great *grá* for competitions. She was one of the organisers of the Feis, which was revived that year after a lapse of many years. I presume she wanted to round up as many competitors as she could. In the early days of the Gaelic League, Feis na Mumhan had been a highly prestigious, annual Gaelic festival. Cork hosted it every year but the festival was never held again after its revival in 1959.

In the Feis that year, which was held in the Sharman Crawford Technical School in Sharman Crawford Street in Cork, there was just one singing competition, open to all adults. Only four men entered. I sang two unaccompanied songs, '*An Clár Bog Déil*' and a lovely Waterford song of emigration called '*Sliabh*

Geal gCua'. On the day, the adjudicator was a great man of music in Cork city named Micheál Ó Ceallacháin. A native of Fermoy, he had a vast knowledge and understanding of Irish traditional music and song. Also, he was the first conductor of the Cork Youth Orchestra, which had been founded only the year before by the Cork Soroptimist Club and held the distinction of being the first youth orchestra in the country. At the end of the competition, Micheál declared me the winner. Later, we became close friends and did many a concert together. At those concerts, he accompanied me on piano and it was a treat to sing with him.

Over the years, I greatly valued Micheál's friendship and the wealth of knowledge he passed on to me about Irish songs and singing. He was a deeply holy and spiritual man, as I learned one summer when we went to Cape Clear Island to give a concert.

On the island, Micheál and I shared a room in the house of Micheál Ó Ceadagáin. Before we went to bed, both of us knelt down to say our night prayers. After saying a quick 'Act of Contrition' and the usual three 'Hail Marys' for holy purity, I hopped into bed. When I woke some hours later, Micheál was still on his knees, praying at the side of his bed. He was a man among men and every now and again I pray to him because he is certainly among the saints of heaven.

Around that time too, I was friendly with Father John O'Neill, the parish priest in Glengarriff. Knowing that I used to sing a bit, Father John invited me to Glengarriff to perform at a fundraiser for a new parochial house he was building. At

Cabaret Gael Linn taken in the Manhattan Hotel, Tralee, at one of the early Rose of Tralee festivals in 1961. Back row (*l–r*): Diarmuid O'Broin, Micheál Ó Conaill, Seán McGuire, Seán and Breandán Ó Dúill; front row (*l–r*): Gráinne NicChormaic, Deirdre Ní Fhloinn, Bláthnaid Ní Gheibheannaigh, Kathleen Watkins and Eibhlín Ní Mharcaight with two members of the audience.

the concert, for the first time, I met Eamon Kelly, the famous *seanchaí* or storyteller. Eamon was married to Máire Ní Shúilleabháin, whose father was a secondary school teacher in Listowel and who was born in Glengarriff. Eamon and Máire happened to be on holiday in the village and, like me, Eamon was roped in to do his bit for the parochial house. Even in those days, Eamon Kelly was a legend and it was a great thrill for me to meet him.

Before the following Lent, Paddy O'Sullivan contacted me. He owned the Rainbow Ballroom in Ballincollig and ran variety concerts over the Lenten period to fill the void caused by Bishop Lucey's ban on Lenten dancing. When Paddy booked Eamon Kelly to do a nine-night tour of Munster, Eamon suggested that he should sign me up as one of his supporting cast. Paddy and I struck a deal – as I recall it was for £3 a night – and a few weeks later on a Saturday night, I headed off with a group of Cork artists to support Eamon in the Carnegie Hall in Kenmare.

That night, for the first time, I met people like Billa O'Connell, a marvellous comedian and pantomime dame beloved of all Corkonians, Frank Fitzpatrick, who was a wonderful accordion player, and a great Irish dancer named Marion White. Many years later, Marion's son Stephen O'Brien was one of the main men on the powerful Cork football All-Ireland winning team of the late 1980s. The cast for the concert also included my good friend John O'Shea.

For my contribution, I usually sang two songs in the first half and two more in the second half. At the time, my repertoire included 'The Irish Soldier Boy', 'The Maid with the Bonny Brown Hair', 'The Scottish Soldier' and a Percy French song, 'Whistling Phil McHugh'. Being hopelessly shy, I stood ramrod straight and shaking in my boots for the entire length of my performance. Looking back on it now, I wonder how I managed to persist at all. However, slowly but surely, I learned to cope as I stood at the side of the stage night after night and watched how Billa engaged the audience. Another fine comedian and compère at that time was Paddy Cotter, who had a wonderfully wry sense of humour and a very subtle approach to comedy.

Although I learned much from Billa, Paddy and others, the man who really taught me the ropes was John O'Shea. He always strolled onto the stage with a big smile on his face and strummed his guitar as he introduced his first song. During each and every performance, he enthralled the audience with a mixed repertoire of country and western songs, Irish ballads and other popular songs, such as Burl Ives' famous folk song 'A Little Bitty Tear'. With John, that great invisible wall at the front of the stage, which can sometimes come between a singer and his audience, just tumbled down. Indeed, if John had been more ambitious about his singing career, there would have been no limit to what he might have achieved. But for him, it was all for the love of singing.

On the dance scene, *céilí* dancing or *céilí* and old-time dancing were popular and many fine *céilí* bands played all over the country, with the most famous of all being the Gallowglass Céilí Band from Naas in County Kildare. They enjoyed huge national and international success and regularly toured abroad, mainly in England, Scotland and America. In Cork, we had two particularly fine *céilí* bands: the Donal Ring Céilí Band; and the Blarney Céilí Band, which was my own favourite.

While most *céilí* bands looked for inspiration to the great Jimmy Shand Band from Scotland, the Blarney Céilí Band were a little different as they played a lot of Irish double reels in their programmes. So, I was really happy when at some festival or other I bumped into the leader of the Blarney Céilí Band, John Murphy, and he invited me to do some dates with the band. Needless to say, I jumped at the opportunity. As a vocalist with a *céilí* band, I would be expected to sing songs for old-time waltzes and military two steps and the odd Gay Gordons, often singing as many as thirty songs each night.

Over the next seven or eight years, I did many gigs with the band. They were a great bunch of multi-talented musicians and came from all over County Cork. John Murphy, the leader, lived in Blackstone Bridge on the outskirts of Cork city and came originally from Lioscarragáin – near Carraig an Ime – which is also the birth place of An tAthair Peadar Ó Laoire, the author of such books as *Séadhna* and *Mo Scéal Féin*. A great fiddler, John had an endless selection of reels, jigs, polkas and hornpipes. Dan Coakley from Ballinagree near Macroom played the three-row accordion and excelled at dance tunes. I often thought of him as the heartbeat of the band. The band's two-row accordionist was Donal Coleman from Grenagh. Like Dan, he was a great player of dance music. On piano accordion, we had Noel Crowley from the Glasheen Road area of Cork city. In any *céilí* band, the purpose of the piano accordionist was to embellish with chords the work of the button accordionists and Noel did that to perfection. At that time, most *céilí* bands included a saxophonist. In our band, an army man named Jerry Casey, from Barrack Street in Cork, filled that role. His father Michael wrote the famous song 'Mick McGilligan's Ball', while Jerry himself composed 'Cork my Home' for Cork 800, which celebrated the 800th

Seán in full voice with his good friends (*l–r*) John R. O'Shea and Billa O'Connell in June 1990 at Cork City Hall. COURTESY MIKE ENGLISH.

anniversary of the granting of a royal charter to the city of Cork. The band also featured bass player Sergeant Jack Rochford, who was based in Collins Barracks in Cork and was the deputy conductor of the Number Two Army Band. The drummer was Joe Terry, a genial man who hailed from Albert Road in the city. Interestingly enough, during the summer season, Joe played with the house band at the Great Southern Hotel in Parknasilla along with Seán Ó Riada, who played the piano.

Every Sunday night and on the odd weeknight too, I headed off with the Blarney Céilí Band in a red and white Volkswagen mini bus. Together, we toured the highways and byways of Munster. All the band's musicians were honest, straightforward guys who played music for the few bob but more so for the fun and camaraderie surrounding it. As a group, they were the best of company and I enjoyed them more than any other group I ever performed with over the years.

As well as singing with the Blarney Céilí Band, I took on other performances too and teamed up with Dan Coakley, the three-row accordionist with the band. We played some memorable concerts in such diverse halls as the Liverpool Philharmonic Hall, the Portmagee Community Centre, Jerry Maidhc Mór's Hall in Ballyvourney, the Gaiety Theatre in Dublin and Power's Hall in Adrigole. Over time, Dan became my regular and only accompanist for solo concerts, and one of my closest friends too, a friendship I value to this day. Indeed, many are the times in my life when I had a problem that I sought and willingly got the wise advice of Dan Coakley.

Around that time too, I made a few guest appearances with The Muskerry Céilí Band and it was there I met John White. John was born in Clonakilty and now he lives with his wife Breeda near Blarney. When the Muskerry band disbanded John

Seán with his great friend and fellow performer John White at an event
for Mallow Senior Citizens in Mallow Library, County Cork, in 2010.

embarked on a solo career as a one-man-band, in other words
a singer who accompanies himself, usually on keyboards. John
has a lovely baritone voice and sings and plays a wide range of
music. *Céilís*, weddings, concerts, church music or cabaret are
no bother to John. I have had the good fortune to do a good

deal of work with him in places like Dunmore House Hotel near Clonakilty and The Ouvane Falls Lounge in Ballylickey. But the most enjoyable gigs we did were in England, mainly in Irish clubs. He is a fine accompanist: throw the man any key and he will stick to you like a leech. As well as the gigs there were all the journeys up and down the motorways and all the discussions on such diverse subjects as 'life hereafter' and 'the healing powers of apple cider vinegar'. John swears by it!

At that time also, I became involved with Gael Linn – a non-governmental, non-profit organisation founded in 1953 to promote the Irish language and arts. I worked with a group called Cabaret Gael Linn. We performed together at all the Great Southern Hotels, which were the leading hotels in the country and were situated along the west coast, in places such as Killarney, Kenmare, Parknasilla, Galway and Bundoran. For each performance, we dressed formally and put on a stylish, fast-moving show for the residents of those up-market hotels.

During my time with the Gael Linn Cabaret, the group featured many well-known performers, such as: Seán McGuire from Belfast, the finest fiddle player of his generation; two fine singing harpists Deirdre Ní Fhloinn and Kathleen Watkins, whom the American tourists adored; and the leading Irish dancer of her day Gráinne Ní Chormaic.

One evening, Deirdre rang me and said that Gael Linn had asked us both to perform that night at the Great Southern Hotel in Killarney. She was told that we were the perfect pair to perform for an important hotel guest and that dinner would be served to us as part of the deal. The name of the special guest was withheld.

Full of excitement and curiosity, Deirdre and I made tracks for Killarney. When we arrived at the hotel, we learned that the important guest was none other than President Éamon de Valera, my childhood hero, whom I had last met in Ballylickey when I was a youngster. Earlier that day, he visited the nuns at the Poor Clare convent in Kenmare, who were celebrating the centenary of their arrival in the town.

Coming from a strong Fianna Fáil family myself – indeed my uncle Mort was known to speak at chapel gates in favour of Fianna Fáil at election times – to sing for de Valera, the last of the nineteen commanders to surrender at Boland Mills in 1916, was for me the ultimate achievement. To put it another way, if I won an Oscar, it would be very much in the halfpenny place in comparison to singing for Dev.

On the night, Deirdre and I performed in the lobby of the hotel for the president, his *aide-de-camp*, his secretary Mairtín O'Flatharta and other residents. For my part, I chose songs that I thought de Valera would enjoy, including 'Boolavogue', 'The West Awake' and 'Seán Ó Duibhir'.

After the performance, the president invited Deirdre and myself to his room for tea and sandwiches. He spoke to us in Irish and made us feel very welcome indeed. Years later, when I happened to meet Mairtín O'Flatharta, secretary to the president, at the funeral of Seán Ó Riada, he praised our performance and said that one of de Valera's favourite songs was 'Boolavogue'.

Shortly after singing for de Valera, Pádraig Tyers, who managed the Cork office of Gael Linn, suggested that I should send a demo tape to the Gael Linn headquarters in Dublin, with a view to making a record. Immediately, I thought of the song I had heard Dónal Ó Mulláin sing all those years ago in Coláiste Íosagáin, '*An Poc ar Buile*'.

As it happened, Deirdre Ní Fhloinn was living in Cork at the time. She was a most generous and helpful person and with her help we made the demo tape of '*An Poc ar Buile*'.

In those days, Gael Linn did great work in recording Irish traditional singers and I hoped against hope that they might include me among their recording artists. The man with the power to decide this was the deputy director of Gael Linn, Roibeárd MacGabhráin, whom I knew through the Gael Linn Cabaret. Sadly, Roibeárd has since passed to his eternal reward but the work he did for the Irish language and music stands as his enduring legacy. After sending off the demo, word quickly came back that Roibeárd was indeed in favour of recording '*An Poc ar Buile*'.

Roibeárd invited me to his home in Stillorgan in Dublin on the following Saturday to audition for Seán Ó Riada, to see if he would have any interest in producing the proposed record. By then, Seán Ó Riada was famous as the composer of the music for *Mise Éire*, the documentary film by George Morrison about the Easter Rising of 1916 and the declaration of independence and the founding of the Republic of Ireland. While I was excited at the thought of meeting such a great composer and musician, I was extremely nervous about auditioning for him.

Shortly after I landed at Roibeárd's house, a big, green Jaguar pulled up outside. Seán Ó Riada stepped out, with his hair tossing in the wind, smoke rising from a big cigar and a gabardine raincoat tightly belted around his waist. Roibeárd led him inside and introduced him to me.

He settled himself down and slowly sipped a whiskey as he listened to me singing '*An Clár Bog Déil*'. I considered it to be my lucky song, especially because it was one of the two songs with which I had won Feis na Mumhan.

On the very first line, Seán raised his hand and stopped me. He told me that I was singing a sanitised version of the song, as the words I sang stated that the man in question would marry the woman of his dreams without a fortune if he had her parents' permission. In Seán's view, there wouldn't be much credit due to the man if he wed the girl only with her parents' consent. Instead, the real proof of his love would be if he married her without their permission. With a smile, Seán suggested that I must have learned the song from one of the books of Seán Óg Ó Tuama. Seán Óg was a saintly man who had a hugely successful radio programme called *Claisceadal an Raidió* and he may well have been the sanitiser. Having heeded Seán's comments, I took up where I had left off and finished the song.

Thankfully, Seán must have liked what he heard because there and then he decided that we should head off in his Jaguar to Peter Hunt's studio in St Stephen's Green and put down four demo tracks, among them '*An Poc ar Buile*'.

Singing to the piano accompaniment of Seán Ó Riada was quite an experience for me. The way in which his playing complemented each song filled me with appreciation and admiration of this genius, as each note and chord he played had a beauty all of its own. That memorable recording session marked the beginning of a deep friendship with Seán and indeed with his wife Ruth, and with their children also; a friendship I am happy to say continues to this very day.

9

SEÁN Ó RIADA AND CEOLTÓIRÍ CHUALANN

Shortly after our first meeting, Seán Ó Riada invited me to take part in a Comhchaidreamh concert in the Foxhall Hotel in Raheny in Dublin, later known as The Old Shieling Hotel, a famous ballad venue. On the night, I sang 'Cath Chéim an Fhia', 'An Clár Bog Déil' and 'The Boys of Kilmichael', which was a great favourite of Seán's. The line-up included the fiddler Seán McGuire, whom I had performed with during my time with the Gael Linn Cabaret, as well as a young, slim, banjo player named Barney McKenna, who later found fame with The Dubliners.

Again, I revelled in performing with Seán Ó Riada as it was an absolute joy to sing to his accompaniment. Above all else, what marked him out from other accompanists was the fact that he tailored his accompaniment totally to support the singer's interpretation of the song. He was so good that I felt he could anticipate any mistakes I might make and cover them up. Now, I look back on that night as being one of the most significant nights of my life. Here was a man who could inspire me to reach a level of performance I thought I would never be capable of achieving.

That night too, I saw for the first time an impish, humorous, almost childlike side of Seán. That very day, he had flown in to Dublin from America and for the concert he wore a spectacular pair of cowboy boots, which had been presented to him in America. As he introduced each item, he sat with his left leg propped up on his right knee to make sure we could all see and, of course, admire his boots.

After the performance, Seán invited me to stay at his Georgian house in Galloping Green on the Stillorgan Road in Dublin, where I met his wife Ruth for the first time. She had a continental air about her, maybe because her mother was Italian. Like Seán, Ruth was born in Cork. Her father was well known in the city and owned the Lido Cinema in the suburb of Blackpool. At Galloping Green, it was plain to see that Ruth and Seán were best friends and soul mates and that she was his strength and support. On the following morning I was hugely impressed when Seán and Ruth's children, Peadar, Rachel, Eoin and Alasdair, brought me breakfast in bed in various instalments.

Strange as it may seem, Irish traditional music had not been Seán Ó Riada's first love. While a student at University College Cork, he had played with dance orchestras in the city, such as

Pat Crowley's Dance Orchestra, the foremost dance band at the time in Cork. He was a good jazz pianist too. Even after he became immersed in Irish traditional music, he loved to play jazz. Often, if he turned up at the RTÉ studios ahead of the other musicians for our recording sessions, he amused himself by playing some jazz on the piano.

When Seán moved to Dublin and took on the job as musical director of the Abbey Theatre in 1957, he became friends with Irish traditional musicians in the city. He was introduced to many of them by Éamon de Buitléar, whom he met when he bought a fishing rod in Hely's game and fishing shop in Dame Street, where Éamon worked. At the time, Éamon was involved in the Irish traditional music scene and encouraged Seán to become involved too. Never a man to do things by half measure, Seán developed a passion for the music and was soon hosting what are now remembered as legendary traditional music sessions in the basement of his home in Galloping Green.

In 1960, for the purpose of providing music for a new play at the Abbey Theatre, *The Song of the Anvil* by Bryan MacMahon, Seán brought together a group of those Irish traditional musicians, rehearsed with them at his home and brought his own particular style to their music. The well-known Irish broadcaster and journalist Seán MacRéamoinn was present at the first rehearsal and wrote, 'What Ó Riada was doing was developing the inner logic of the music and the only parallel I can make is that of jazz where he was giving different instruments their head. They did their break, as it were, but he managed to weld them into a unity. And the sound that emerged, with tunes that many of us knew for a long time, was quite exciting.' The performance of the band was such a success that Ó Riada decided they should continue playing together. And so Ceoltóirí Chualann was born.

The band was launched at the Dublin Theatre Festival in the Shelbourne Hotel at an event called *Reacaireacht an Riadaigh,* or Ó Riada's Recital. The programme also featured traditional singers, the writer Seán Ó Ríordáin and the poet Seán Ó Tuama. At Seán's invitation, almost all of the ministers in government attended the performance. The original members of the group were: John Kelly, a famous fiddle player from Clare based in Dublin, who ran a small haberdashery shop in Capel Street; Sonny Brogan, a legendary and highly-respected Dublin accordionist; Martin Fay, a classically-trained violinist and member of the Abbey Theatre Orchestra; and Éamon de Buitléar, an accomplished musician, who played the mouth organ, bodhrán and button accordion and later became better known as the man who made so many superb television programmes in the Irish language about the environment and nature. Also on board were Seán Potts, who came from a famous Dublin musical family, and played the tin whistle; the flute player Michael Tubridy from Clare; and the *uilleann* piper Paddy Moloney. Finally there was Ronnie McShane, the assistant stage manager at the Abbey Theatre, who played the bones and became the life and soul of the band; and of course, Seán Ó Riada himself completed the line-up on bodhrán. Eventually, Seán switched to the harpsichord and Peadar Mercier took his place on the bodhrán.

Over the years, the membership of the group remained mostly the same but there were a few additions. The great *seannós* singer Darach Ó Catháin, who sang in the Connemara style, frequently featured with the Ceoltóirí and the fiddler Seán Keane joined the band after winning a fiddle competition on *Fleadh Cheoil an Raidió*.

At that time, I was singing with the Blarney Céilí Band and one Sunday night, when I arrived home fairly late from a gig, I found my mother sitting up in bed wide awake. She told me she had heard a band on Radio Éireann the like of which she had never heard before. She said, 'They are a little mad. But I like their music. It was great.' She had tuned in to the first of a series of radio programmes presented by Ó Riada for which he retained the name *Reacaireacht an Riadaigh* and featured Ceoltóirí Chualann and the singing of Darach Ó Catháin. She told me that I should listen to the band. The programme was repeated later in the week and I did tune in. I was bowled over by what I heard. Ceoltóirí Chualann played an arrangement by Seán of that haunting melody 'A Spailpín a Rúin'. The second time around Paddy launched into a pipe solo and at the turn of verse came a wild and powerful drone from the base of Éamon's accordion. Never again would I see Irish music in the same light. Gone was our dependence on Jimmy Shand, no disrespect to him, I loved his music and still do. Later in the programme, Darach Ó Catháin sang Seán Ó Riada's arrangement of *'Peigín Leitir Mhóir'* with Ceoltóirí Chualann. Little did I think that night that I would follow in his footsteps when Darach was forced to emigrate to Leeds in search of work.

When Seán began to present another weekly radio programme *Fleadh Cheoil an Raidió*, he invited me along every now and again to sing on the show. Gradually, I became the resident singer. Eamon Kelly the *seanchaí* also featured on the programme. Eamon was the ultimate perfectionist and he crafted his stories with great skill. I got to know him well. He was a man of great sincerity and integrity, a decent man in every way. *Fleadh Cheoil an Raidió* had a huge listening audience not only in Ireland but in England too. At first, the shows were recorded at St Francis Xavier Hall in Dublin and later at the GPO in Henry Street.

In 1962, Seán Ó Riada composed the score for the film version of *The Playboy of the Western World* and Ceoltóirí Chualann played the soundtrack. That same year, Gael Linn decided that I should record 'An Poc ar Buile' with Seán Ó Riada and Ceoltóirí Chualann. We recorded four songs in the Marion Hall in Milltown in Dublin. In those days, recording was a rather basic operation. A microphone was placed in the middle for the singer and the musicians sat around in a circle with a few more microphones, moving their chairs back and forth until a balance was achieved. All sang and played together until Seán was satisfied that we had got a 'take'. I am sure I must have sung the '*Poc*' twenty times before it was in the can. The record was released as an EP, which means extended play. These records usually had four or five tracks and played at a speed of 45 revolutions per minute. As well as '*An Poc ar Buile*', the EP featured three other songs, 'An Spealadóir', 'Torramh an Bharraile' and 'Amhráinín Siodraimín'.

Straight away, the record became a huge hit, mainly due to the popularity of 'An Poc ar Buile'. Every time I switched on the radio, I seemed to hear myself singing it. In those days, Ireland had no official song charts. But, it's fair to say that the record became an instant hit and was played over and over again on various radio programmes.

In no time at all, offers to perform at concerts and other events came flooding in. I sang at venues all over Ireland. As teaching was still my day job, I performed mostly at weekends. My poor old Morris Minor was run off its feet.

On Easter Sunday night 1965, I sang at an Easter commemoration concert at the Gaiety Theatre in Dublin. After the concert, as I left by the stage door, a man introduced himself to me as Tommy Walsh, the manager of the Irish Centre in Liverpool. He invited me to perform at a concert in England and I accepted on the spot. It would be my first ever appearance outside of Ireland. I asked my good friend and accompanist Dan Coakley to join me for the gig. We decided to travel by air. But, we must have been a little bit anxious about the flight because both of us made our wills before we went. I'm sure we went to Confession as well.

The concert was held at the Liverpool Philharmonic Hall, a beautiful venue. It was the first of hundreds of concerts I did all over England, mainly in Irish clubs in London, Liverpool, Manchester, Derby and Birmingham. One of the most memorable of all was a St Patrick's Day concert in the Royal

Albert Hall in London. This was a monstrous venue with 6,000 seats. The size of it alone scared the living daylights out of me. By then, I was well known among the Irish in England as a singer because of *Fleadh Cheoil an Raidió* and the audiences were reasonably familiar with my repertoire. When I sang '*An Poc ar Buile*', the whole auditorium joined in the chorus to celebrate their national feast day. It was a truly unforgettable experience.

Back home, I found myself in much demand too, especially for performances with Ceoltóirí Chualann, although, like Darach Ó Catháin, I never officially joined the group. As well as recording for radio, Ceoltóirí Chualann appeared on television shows, such as *Aililiú* and *Music and Man*. On the whole, they rarely performed live, though I remember singing with them in concerts in Kilrush, Scarriff, Kenmare and Millstreet.

In March 1969, Roibeárd MacGabhráin, the deputy director of Gael Linn who had introduced me to Seán Ó Riada, decided that the time had come to showcase Seán's music in a concert in the Gaiety Theatre to commemorate the 250th anniversary of the death of the great Ulster poet Peadar Ó Doirnín. *Ó Riada sa Gaiety* was chosen as the title for the concert.

To select the songs for the concert and prepare for the big night, Seán Ó Riada and I met at his home in Coolea, where he had been living for the previous five years or so. We decided to include a few of Ó Doirnín's compositions, among them a setting of his poem '*Mná na hÉireann*'. While working on

Seán with Sir Matt Busby and A.N. Other at Old Trafford around 1979.

the song, I had difficulty learning the air. Like me, Seán was not too enthusiastic about the tune. To this day, I can still remember his words, 'I think I can do better than that.' Up we went to the parlour and Seán sat down at the piano. In less than twenty minutes, he had composed the beautiful air to which '*Mná na hÉireann*' is now sung. In all, about thirty vocal and instrumental recordings of that melody exist, including a memorable one in Irish by Kate Bush and versions by Mike Oldfield, James Last, Phil Coulter and Sinéad O'Connor. Meanwhile, the tickets had gone on sale for the Gaiety concert. They sold out on the first day, a rare feat indeed considering that there was no online booking available in those times.

During his years as leader of Ceoltóirí Chualann, Seán Ó Riada always looked on the group as the national folk orchestra of Ireland. And so, to mark the importance of the commemoration concert, he decided that we should all dress in formal attire.

On the night of the concert, a wonderful sense of occasion pervaded. President Éamon de Valera sat to the right of the stage, while the audience was made up of *maithe agus mór, uaisle na tíre* – the great and the good of Ireland. Thankfully, the performance itself matched the expectation. I suppose, of all the times I have ever sung, this was the *buaic phointe,* the high point. Believe it or not, in my mind I always compared it to the transfiguration, when Jesus took Peter, James and John up to the top of a high mountain and showed them paradise. For me, Ó Riada sa Gaiety was my transfiguration moment.

During the interval, Seán Ó Riada and I were invited to the Green Room. We waited in line to be greeted by the president. As he approached, Seán Ó Riada remarked on de Valera's pale appearance and whispered in my ear that maybe it was time to start on the requiem the government had commissioned him to compose in anticipation of the president's demise. Little did I think that night that Seán himself would depart this planet some years before de Valera.

Without doubt, the concert proved a great personal triumph for Seán and indeed in a lesser way for all of us associated with him. It also resulted in the recording of the album *Ó Riada sa Gaiety*, although the record was not released immediately.

In June 1970, at the Carolan Tercentenary Concert in City Hall in Cork, the original Ceoltóirí Chualann played together for the last time. It was clear that some of the group were anxious to move on, to perform more concerts and go professional and more power to them. Seán Ó Riada, whose day job was lecturing at University College Cork, was not interested in going down that road, neither were John Kelly, Éamon de Buitléar or Ronnie McShane. Seán, I think, felt that he had brought the Ceoltóirí Chualann project as far as he could and so he disbanded the group. For my own part, I wanted to continue teaching, because I liked teaching and also because I valued the security of the weekly pay cheque. Sonny Brogan had by this time passed on to his eternal reward. Paddy Moloney had founded The Chieftains and was joined by Michael Tubridy, Seán Potts, Seán Keane, Martin Fay and Peadar Mercier. Over time, the group became famous worldwide and can take most of the credit for the spread of the popularity of Irish music internationally. Musically they progressed as well, I am thinking in particular about their recording with Tom Jones of 'The Tennessee Waltz'. Yet, it is right to point out that there would be no Chieftains as we know them if Seán Ó Riada had not formed Ceoltóirí Chualann. They are part of Seán Ó Riada's musical legacy. Without doubt, he was the single most influential figure in the revival of Irish traditional music in the 1960s.

Likewise, most of what I myself achieved as a singer is largely due to Seán Ó Riada. Under his influence, I developed as a traditional singer. He gave me the confidence to sing songs in a way that I may not otherwise have attempted. Indeed, I am reminded of one famous occasion when we were recording 'The Banks of my own Lovely Lee' for a documentary film called *Rhapsody of a River* by Louis Marcus, another great Cork man. I found it difficult to follow the score and failed to stay with the orchestra. Knowing that I was in trouble, Seán moved over to my rostrum. In a low voice, he reminded me that our grandfathers had sold bonhams together at Bantry Fair and he advised me not to worry too much about the symphony orchestra. We recorded the song in the next take.

In my mind, nobody can compare to Seán Ó Riada, not only on a professional level, but also as a close and trusted friend.

10

A True Friend

From the very first day that Seán Ó Riada and I met, we felt at ease in each other's company. I think there were a number of similarities in our backgrounds and in our upbringing that contributed to this being so. We were practically the same age, as I was just four years younger than him. We were the children of public servants: our four parents were paid by the State. Seán's father, Seán Reidy from Kilmihil in County Clare, was a Garda Sergeant and his mother, Julia Mary Creedon from Kilnamartyra near Macroom, was a Jubilee nurse, a public health nurse in today's terms. And my parents were teachers.

Like me, growing up as the son of public servants, Seán had felt a little left out when it came to mixing with other children. As a result, he too was shy and introverted in his youth. From an early age, we were both made aware of the importance of education. I remember my father often telling me that he had no farm to leave me and that the books were my only hope. I remember also Seán suggesting to me that we had both benefited from a good education system which left us both well able to make our way in the world and he particularly pointed out that it also gave us a sense of who we were, a respect for our country and a command and a love of our native tongue.

Indeed whenever we were together, we often spoke Irish. For a person who was not a native speaker, Seán had beautiful Irish and a fine Gaeltacht *blas*. His musical ear would have helped him there. When rehearsing with Ceoltóirí Chualann, he always gave the musicians their instructions in English. Yet, he always gave me my instructions in Irish, as if it was the natural language between us.

Another bond between us was that we were both Cork men. At the time of Seán's birth, the family lived in Caherdaniel in County Kerry, where Seán's father was stationed. But Julia Mary made sure that Seán was born in the North Infirmary in Cork city, where she herself had qualified as a nurse. Indeed, during that memorable first meeting at Roibeárd's house, Seán had said that he was pleased to have found a Cork man who could sing 'The Banks of My Own Lovely Lee' for him.

In his heyday, Seán was the toast of the politicians of all political parties. He often badgered them on many issues, such as keeping the schools in his area open or building a new factory in Coolea. They loved to be seen in his company. Regularly, they asked him to make an input into party policies on music or the arts. He always obliged. On one such project, he worked closely with Charles Haughey to bring about tax concessions for artists.

In his own way, Seán was a deeply spiritual person and his highly acclaimed liturgical compositions prove this. To listen to his *Aifreann Chúil Aodha,* recorded with the choir he founded and loved, Cór Chúil Aodha, is for me anyway a spiritual experience in itself. Now and again, if I am feeling a spiritual drought and a difficulty in praying, I listen to the *Aifreann* and I let it do my praying for me. Wherever there are Irish who gather in prayer in this world of ours, Seán's settings of '*Ag Críost an Síol*' and '*Ár nAthair*' are likely to be heard. Maybe this was the greatest of his many achievements.

Shortly after I met Seán, he asked me if I would bring his parents with me from Cork to one of his basement parties in Galloping Green. It turned out to be a great trip and the start of a close and enduring friendship. Seán's parents were that kind of a couple who willingly embraced you and accepted you into their world.

After that trip, I made a point of visiting them every week at their home in the Glasheen suburb of Cork city. After Eileen and I married, we continued to call to see them most Monday nights. Years later, I found out that in her letters to a cousin in America, Seán's mother Julia Mary always referred to me as her 'second son'. And that was exactly how I felt. Julia Mary was a gregarious, extroverted lady who enjoyed nothing more than swapping yarns or knocking the odd tune out of her melodeon. But beneath that exterior was a wise, thrifty, practical woman, a woman of great faith. Her husband played the fiddle, which he learned from Patrick Kelly of Cree, and was deeply religious also. He was a quiet, reserved, gentle person but I often felt there was steel behind it which served him well in his career as a Garda. He was one of the first group of men to leave the Garda Depot after the Civil War. Ireland owes a huge debt to these unarmed men who established law and order in this state.

Usually, before recording programmes, Seán and I practiced at his home in Coolea. Most times, I brought his parents along with me. They would sit in the parlour talking to Ruth and the children while we rehearsed in the studio. More often than not, near the end of a session, Seán would suggest that we should move up to the parlour to practice a song at the piano. Somehow, I always thought this was also for the benefit of his parents. Finally, when the rehearsal finished, we would all sit around a roaring fire, sipping tea and chatting and usually telling a few jokes.

On the way home to Cork, Seán's mother Julia Mary would ask me to sing one of the songs she had heard me practice with Seán. She might interrupt and say, 'Now, the lad had a nice twist there. You haven't got it right yet.' She loved listening to songs and music. She had a keen ear and always said that Seán had a special touch on the piano that she would recognise anywhere. Her comment to her husband would always be, 'Dad, the boyo has the touch.' They were both extremely proud of their son, as well they might be.

As a person, Seán Ó Riada was totally different to the man I had been expecting to meet that day in Roibeárd's house. People had told me that he could be awkward and difficult to work with. I found he was the direct opposite. When we

Seán with Liam Clancy at a Saturday night dance at the Arcadia Ballroom in 1962. The Clancys and Tommy Makem made a guest appearance. This was just after Seán had recorded '*An Poc Ar Buile*'.
COURTESY *IRISH EXAMINER*.

Ceoltóirí Chualann on stage for Ó Riada sa Gaiety in March 1969, (*l–r*): Seán Ó Riada, Peadar Mercier, Éamon de Buitléar, Martin Fay, Seán Keane, John Kelly, Seán Potts, Michael Tubridy and Paddy Moloney. Seán is at the front. COURTESY GAEL LINN.

Meeting the President at the Ó Riada sa Gaiety Concert, March 1969, (*l–r*): Seán Ó Riada, Seán, Niall Toibín, President Éamon de Valera, Ruth Ó Riada and Breandán Ó Buachalla. Courtesy Gael Linn.

Seán with Seán Ó Riada and Niall Toibín at the Gaiety Dublin for Ó Riada sa Gaiety. Courtesy Gael Linn.

David O'Loghlin of Circa Records presents Seán with a Silver Record for his LP *The Banks of My Own Lovely Lee*, June 1973. Circa Records recorded the LP, which was arranged and produced by Cathal Dunne.

Seán with Matthew Allen in Cork. Matthew is an ethnomusicologist who teaches at Wheaton College, a university of the arts near Boston in the US.

In December 2008, President Mary McAleese hosted a series of three RTÉ radio discussions from Áras an Uachtaráin in which both Seán and Gabriel Byrne took part.

Seán with Dr Martin and President Mary McAleese at Áras an Uachtaráin, December 2008.

Seán sings at the reception in Bantry to celebrate when the Cork footballers brought the Sam Maguire Cup to the town in 2010. Graham Canty from Bantry, pictured in the blue shirt, was team captain for the victory. COURTESY *IRISH EXAMINER*.

Seán, MC, and Peadar Ó Riada backstage during the 'Music from Muskerry/Ceol ó Mhúscraí' launch concert in the Briery Gap, Macroom, in aid of the paediatric leukaemia unit of the Mercy Hospital in 2010. Picture: Richard Mills. COURTESY *IRISH EXAMINER*.

Seán singing with Con and Áine at the recording of the TG4 programme *Seán Ó Sé – An Pocar* at Coughlan's Public House in Douglas Street, Cork, December 2013.

Seán with his family in April 2015. Back row (*l–r*): his daughter-in-law Caitríona, son Con, daughters Íde and Áine and granddaughter Méabh; front row (*l–r*): his grandson Seán, sister Maureen, Seán, granddaughter Ciara and wife Eileen. COURTESY PEADAR FORBES.

worked together for performances, he showed great patience and understanding of any problems that I came up against. Somehow, I felt he saw me as a person who was reliable, as I stuck to my role, which was to learn, practice and perform to the best of my ability the songs he selected for me. At all times, he was very much for my good and looked out for me.

One night, while doing a concert in Dublin, I was feeling tired after a long day of rehearsing and singing. Somebody offered me some kind of pep pill and put me under some pressure to take it. Straight away, Seán stepped forward and told him to leave me alone.

Unlike Seán, I was a Pioneer. He respected me for that. At a party one night, a particular guy who had drunk too much tried to force a pint into my hand. Again, Seán got annoyed and said, 'God damn it, can't you see he has a Pioneer pin on his coat? Leave him alone.'

He was so busy with so many things that meeting deadlines was often a bit of a problem for him and yet I cannot remember him missing one; he always managed to deliver, sometimes just in the nick of time.

On the night before we were due to record the soundtrack for the film *Kennedy's Ireland*, an account of JFK's visit to Ireland, which was to include songs such as 'Boolavogue' and 'Kelly the Boy from Killane', we practiced together in Coolea. After viewing parts of the film, Seán turned to me and said of the proposed theme song, 'I don't like that song "Goodbye Mick Goodbye Pat". It's a bit stage Irish. I must contact Charles Davis and try and change it.' Now Charles

Davis was the director and producer of the film and he lived in Hollywood. Off we went to Coolea and walked into the post office and Seán asked the postmaster Dónal Ó Scanaill to put him through to Charles Davis in Hollywood and called out a number with about fourteen digits. This was no small task for the unfortunate Dónal. But, finally having negotiated seven or eight telephone exchanges, Charles Davis picked up his phone in his Hollywood home. He understood Sean's dilemma and proposed 'The Shores of Amerikay' instead. Seán readily accepted.

All was well until we sat into the car and Seán suddenly realised that he was not terribly familiar with either the melody or lyrics of the new song. We were in a fix now, having given up a song we knew for one we didn't know, with the recording due to take place on the following day. Then I happened to think of Mike Murphy from Blackstone Bridge, the father of John, the leader of the Blarney Céilí Band. Even though Mike was well into his eighties, I was convinced that he would know the words and air of the song. The same man, God bless him, knew every song I ever heard of.

Without delay, I jumped into my car and headed for Blackstone Bridge near Blarney where Mike lived. Mike knew only the first verse and I recorded him singing it on tape. But, as luck would have it, after much searching in the attic, he finally located the entire words of the song in an old edition of *Ireland's Own*.

Straight away, I headed back to Coolea and left the tape with Seán, who immediately began to orchestrate the melody for the following morning's recording with the Symphony Orchestra. I went back to Cork as dawn was breaking, hopped on the first train to Dublin and learned the song on the journey. I took a taxi to the Xavier Hall and as I walked in the door I heard the melodious strains of the orchestra as Seán brought them through their paces with his new arrangement of 'The Shores of Amerikay'.

Ironically, following the assassination of President Kennedy, the film never went on general release but it is screened every day at the John F. Kennedy Museum and Library at Colombia Point in Boston.

Over the years, Seán and I travelled a lot together, up and down the country by car. All the way, going and coming, we chatted non-stop and swapped yarns. For six months of the year, we drove from Cork to Dublin and home again to record *Fleadh Cheoil an Raidió*. No matter how long or how short the journey, he was always great company, as he was a captivating storyteller. When we'd drive home from Dublin, he could start a story at Newlands Cross in Clondalkin and mightn't finish it until we got to the Dunkettle Roundabout in Cork.

He showed interest in almost everything under God's earth, from science fiction to sailing. He was a voracious reader of science fiction and actually wrote science fiction reviews for *The Irish Times.* His mind was never idle. He always had several ideas spinning around in his head, all at the same time, such as making a film, writing a musical, building an airstrip or setting up a new industry for Coolea. Although he had plenty of knowledge to back up each and every plan, he rarely considered the practicalities. Deep down, he was a dreamer.

One evening, we were strolling together in a marshy area by the Sulán River in Coolea. Seán said that he'd had a plan – a 'dream' might be a better word – to build a high-rise hotel on that exact spot, with a helipad on the roof. He believed it would attract anglers and fowlers from all over Europe who could be flown into Cork airport and then ferried to Coolea by helicopter. Full of enthusiasm, he mentioned the idea to his friend Liam Browne from Killarney. Being a realist, Liam saw the pitfalls straight away and pointed out to Seán that building a hotel in the middle of a marsh would be a bit of a problem, not to mind raising the finance for such a daft idea. That was the end of that particular scheme.

Sadly, soon afterwards, Seán was struck by a serious illness. As his health began to decline, so too all his hopes and dreams began to fade away slowly.

11

FAREWELL TO SEÁN

When Seán Ó Riada became seriously ill in the summer of 1971, he was admitted as a patient to the Bon Secours Hospital in Cork. At the time, I did not realise how ill he was and I had no notion of what lay ahead.

Yet, when I visited him at the Bons, I could see that he was not getting any better, indeed he was getting worse. So it came as no surprise to me when I learned that he was being transferred to the King's College Hospital in London in a last desperate attempt to save his life.

To begin his journey, Seán was taken by private ambulance to Cork Airport. An Aer Lingus plane was diverted from Shannon Airport to take him to London. To make room on the plane for his stretcher, about five rows of seats had to be removed.

On the day of Seán's departure from the airport, someone rang me at school to tell me that a problem had arisen, as the private ambulance firm had refused to let their stretcher go with Seán to London. I decided to go to the airport but on my way I stopped to phone my good friend John O'Shea, who was on duty at the Cork Fire Station. John arranged to get a stretcher from the Cork Fire Brigade and he took it to the airport without delay.

As Seán was wheeled out to the runway on the stretcher, I walked beside him to the steps of the plane. We spoke no goodbyes. He knew and I knew that we would not meet again on this earth. In that strange telepathic manner, we took leave of one another. To use a well worn cliché, for me it was the day the music stopped.

At King's College Hospital, Seán was put under the care of Nurse O'Sullivan, a staff nurse from Beara who was a fluent Irish speaker. Afterwards, she said that Seán had such an acute awareness and knowledge of his illness that he was able to give a detailed account of how he felt and that the information he gave was useful in subsequently treating his condition in others with similar problems.

While in King's College, Seán had many visitors, among them An Taoiseach Jack Lynch and Bishop Eamon Casey whom he had known since childhood.

Every day, I spoke by phone to Seán's sister Louise. She had gone to London to be with Seán, along with her husband the artist Walter Verling and Seán's wife Ruth, who was bravely battling cancer herself. The fact that Seán and Ruth were both gravely ill must have caused them untold grief and sorrow, especially as they had seven young children: Peadar; Rachel; Eoghan; Alasdair; Cathal; Sorcha; and the youngest child

Seán and Eileen, and Páidí Ó Lionáird in the background, at Seán and
Ruth Ó Riada's grave in 2009.

Liadh, who was only four years of age. As well as making
contact every day with Louise, I visited Seán's parents daily to
keep them up to date with his condition.

On Saturday night, 3 October 1971, while I was at Union
Hall for a concert, my wife Eileen phoned to tell me the sad
news that Seán had passed away. He was only forty years of

age. I was asked to let his parents know of his death early the next morning, before they might hear it on the eight o'clock news.

On the following morning at half past seven, I called to Seán's parents' house in Dorgan's Road in Cork city. His mother Julia Mary opened the door. Ever before I spoke, she said, 'You don't have to tell me anything. I feel the boyo is gone.' Putting her hand on her heart, she said, 'Go over to the church and get Dad. He's gone to eight o'clock Mass.' I went over to the Church of the Immaculate Conception for Seán. I found him deep in prayer and I brought him home.

Later, I took both Seán and Julia Mary back to our own house. I have never in my life seen such an outpouring of faith and acceptance as I saw on that day.

In the afternoon, I drove them to Coolea to see their grandchildren. The two of them sat together in the back seat of the car and spent the entire journey reciting rosaries.

Some days later, when Seán's mortal remains arrived at Cork Airport, accompanied by Ruth, Louise and Walter, over a thousand people had gathered there to welcome him home, among them his children.

As the funeral cortège slowly made its lonesome journey west along the Lee Valley towards Coolea, people stood at every crossroad to pay their respects. Hundreds of cars followed the procession, on through Coachford, Macroom and Ballyvourney. Shops closed their doors and crowds lined the roads, bowing their heads in silent prayer as the cortège passed. The crowds grew larger as the cavalcade of cars passed by the

Sulán River, where we remembered Seán's beautiful, evocative arrangement of that fine air 'The Banks of Sulán'.

When we reached his adoptive home place, Coolea, it seemed as if the whole population had turned up to grieve his passing, to salute and celebrate his life and to comfort his widow Ruth and their young family. They came too to sympathise with his elderly mother Julia Mary, who was one of their own, a member of the Creedon family from nearby Kilnamartyra, and with his father Seán. They mourned him as a clan would mourn a fallen chieftain. In truth, he was their *gile mear,* their hero. As Professor Aloysius Fleischmann said so aptly, his homecoming resembled that of a king coming back among his own people. Finally, the cortège arrived at St Gobnait's church in Coolea, where Father Donncha Ó Conchúir received Sean's mortal remains.

On the following day, at one o'clock, Father Donncha celebrated the funeral Mass in the presence of the bishop of Cloyne, Bishop John Ahern, and a packed congregation, among them Charles Haughey and General Tom Barry. An amplifier allowed the crowds outside to follow the proceedings. Although I had been asked to sing at the Mass, I declined, as I was too emotional. Willie Clancy, Tony MacMahon and Ceoltóirí Chualann all played and Cór Chúil Aodha, now directed by Seán's son Peadar, plaintively sang the Mass composed by their founder.

After Mass, the piper Alf Kennedy led the funeral procession to St Gobnait's cemetery, 3 miles away. Thousands of mourners walked the whole distance behind an empty hearse as the coffin was shouldered all the way. As Seán's coffin was lowered into the ground, his mother Julia Mary, who had accepted her son's death with great courage, turned to me and said, 'I know now that there is no suffering worse than the death of one of your own children.'

Following Seán's burial, I was leaving the graveyard with his mother and father when John Kelly of Ceoltóirí Chualann joined us. As he gently embraced Julia Mary, speaking of Seán, he said to her, 'Mrs, he raised us all up.' Indeed he did.

The whole nation mourned the passing of Seán Ó Riada and the thousands who attended his removal and funeral gave testimony to the special place he held in the hearts of the Irish people.

Following Seán's death, the album *Ó Riada sa Gaiety* was finally released. Strangely, one of Seán's last compositions had been a Requiem Mass that was commissioned by RTÉ and broadcast for the first time in 1975 on the death of President Éamon de Valera.

I think of Seán every day. I miss him every day. I pray for him and I pray to him.

12

LOVE AND LOSS

In between all the concerts and gigs, I still found time to go dancing and always enjoyed the ballroom scene and particularly the showbands.

One Sunday night in August 1966, I headed off on my own to the Redbarn Ballroom near Youghal. The summer holidays had ended, a new school year was on the horizon and I may have been a little bit down in myself that yet another – as I remember it – glorious summer had passed by.

On the night, The Dixies showband took to the stage and their lead singer Brendan O'Brien belted out all the latest pop songs, among them his hits, 'Little Arrows' and 'It Doesn't Matter Anymore'. When he announced a quick step, somehow or other I found myself with my back to the wall on the women's side of the hall. A huge mass of men surged forward. In the shove, an unfortunate girl was pushed up against me and firmly planted her stiletto on my left shoe. I'm sure I uttered some kind of awful obscenity, then regretted it and asked the same girl out for a dance. We got talking and I learned that she was Eileen Tangney from Knockane in east Cork, halfway between Killeagh and Castlemartyr. At the time, she was working in the Munster and Leinster Bank in Charleville. I took her out for a few more dances and finally plucked up the courage and made a date for the following Wednesday night. We went to a film in Limerick and we later found out that neither of us were really cinema goers. Indeed, we've scarcely been to a film together since.

In January 1967, Eileen and I got engaged and we married on 26 July in Killeagh, with Seán Ó Riada as my best man and Eileen's sister Bríd as her bridesmaid. The officiating priest was my first cousin Father Seán O'Shea, my Uncle Paddy's son from Castletownbere, and I am glad to report that he is still hale and hearty at the ripe old age of ninety-two. Thankfully, Eileen and I were blessed with three beautiful, healthy children, Áine, Con and Íde, all of whom were adored by my mother. When our son Con arrived, she had been widowed for sixteen years and she was particularly happy to have another Con Ó Sé in the family.

After moving to Cork in 1961, my mother got a new lease of life and took much pleasure in her retirement. Every morning, she headed to the city on the ten o'clock bus and went to Mass at eleven o'clock in St Augustine's church. Later, she strolled over to Thompson's café for tea and buns with her retired teacher cronies. She enjoyed a bit of gardening and even mowed the front lawn now and again. She loved needle work and knitting too and made some lovely Fair Isle jumpers,

Seán and Eileen sign the wedding register at the Parish Church, Killeagh, County Cork, on 26 July 1967. Father Seán O'Shea, Seán's first cousin, married them.

Eileen and Áine taken at home in 1969.

Growing up (*l–r*): Eileen, Íde, Áine, Con and Seán, taken at home *c.* spring 1977.

the knitting of which required much concentration due to the many colours used.

One evening in February 1977, as I was having a haircut in Gerry Burns' in Parnell Place, my sister Maureen rang the shop to say that she had come home and found my mother dead in her bed, with a cup of tea and a slice of toast beside her.

In contrast to my father at the time of his passing, my mother looked extremely calm. Maureen and I believe that she died peacefully in her sleep, which gave us some comfort. We brought her back to Bantry and buried her beside my father, whom she had loved dearly all her life.

After the final prayers, as I walked with Eileen and my sister Maureen out through the iron gates of the cemetery, fond memories of my mother came flooding back, such as tuning in to Lord Haw Haw, treating her friend Katie Bracken to high tea and busily going from shop to shop in Bantry on a Saturday evening. In my mind, I could hear her once more singing 'The Gypsy's Warning', which had always been her favourite song.

13

St Mary's on the Hill

Despite all the singing, teaching took up most of my life and even more so in 1971 when I became principal of the Cathedral Boys' National School.

Further up the hill from the school, Cork city continued to expand and a new suburb began to emerge in the late 1970s and early 1980s. During that time, Cork Corporation built more than 1,200 new houses in Knocknaheeny, which was less than a mile away from the Cathedral school. Despite its proximity and the fact that Knocknaheeny belonged to the Cathedral parish, I knew next to nothing about the development there.

One day, a priest whom I had never met before knocked on my classroom door and introduced himself as Father Con White, the new curate in Knocknaheeny. He asked me if I might help with a new church choir he was forming. At the time, the church in Knocknaheeny was not yet built and so Mass was said every Sunday in the local community school. Without giving it a second thought, I threw my lot in with the choir. I quickly grew to admire this fledgling community as they sought to put down their roots in this corner of the old Cathedral parish, the North parish as it was usually called.

At that time, the administrator of the Cathedral parish was Canon Denis O'Connor from Dromore near Bantry. One night, after some meeting or other, he asked me if I would be interested in applying for the post of principal in the new national school in Knocknaheeny, the building of which had already got underway. There and then, I told him that I would indeed be interested. In due course, the post was advertised and I applied. Following an interview I was appointed.

Being principal of any school is a daunting task but in a new school it involves much more work and planning. I suppose I was a little bit apprehensive about the whole undertaking. However, a short time later, my morale was greatly boosted when my good friend and colleague Liz Nolan, who was vice principal with me in the Cathedral school, was appointed to the same post in the new school. I knew she would do an excellent job in Knocknaheeny and so she did. The initial enrolment allowed the appointment of one other assistant teacher and the successful applicant for this post was Nuala Healy, a young teacher from Aghabullogue near Coachford. Over the years, I came to know her as a wonderful teacher and a loyal colleague and I am glad and happy to say that she is still one of my closest friends.

On 1 September 1980, the school opened in a rented premises belonging to the community school, with two junior infant classes and a total enrolment of eighty pupils.

Founding staff of St Mary's on the Hill National School,
Knocknaheeny, Cork city, July 1980, (l–r): Liz Nolan,
Father Con White, Nuala Kelleher (née Healy) and Seán.

In the following year, we moved to our new state-of-the-art school. By this time, Knocknaheeny was a parish known as St Mary's on the Hill. Father White was now the parish priest and he suggested the school should be known as St Mary's on the Hill National School. More often than not, we used the Irish version of the name, also suggested by Father White, Scoil Mhuire ar Chnoc na hAoine. I liked that name very much. The school grew rapidly and in 1983 we added another eight classrooms.

For a school to be successful, all the various members of the school community have to work together and trust each other. By that I mean that the Board of Management, the Department of Education, the principal, the staff, including the secretary and the school caretaker, and most of all the parents, must all pull together for the good of the children and work to ensure that the children reach their full potential. I think this happened in Knocknaheeny. Our school secretary, Deirdre O'Shea, came from nearby Fairhill and I must acknowledge all the help and loyalty she gave me during our time together. She looked after much of the routine administration and was an expert at coping with the mountains of paperwork involved. Incidentally, her father, Christy O'Shea, was one of the 'Shea boys' clan and is often mentioned as one of the best Cork hurlers who never won an All-Ireland medal.

At its peak, enrolment in St Mary's on the Hill reached 927 pupils. Ideally, I don't think that a national school should be that big. However, when everybody cooperates, much can be done and I believe that much was done in Knocknaheeny.

St Mary's on the Hill National School staff outing *c.* 1984 (*l–r*): Seán Horgan, Nuala Healy, Liz Nolan, Margaret O'Shea, Claire O'Shea, Ursula McCarthy, Ger Lawton, Patricia O'Donovan, Seán, Marjorie Flynn (behind Seán), Colette O'Driscoll, Catherine Shanahan (at far back beside Marjorie), Marese Spencer, Michelle Healy, Mary Halbert, Seán Ó Murchú, Noreen Meaney and Lorraine Downey. COURTESY GER O'DONOVAN.

The core population of this new, diverse community was made up of sons and daughters of people who had lived on the northside of the city. Many other residents came from outside the city and some were not used to urban living. Naturally, those people found it hard to settle in to life in a built-up area.

From the outset, Father White was extremely involved in the community. A caring and active priest, he helped people fight for their rights and also put down roots. The area had no formal community council. Yet, under the leadership of Father White, much progress was made.

Side by side with Father White, the school played an active role in the development of the community. My colleagues and I attended many local meetings. We organised lectures for the community on various topics and liaised with An Garda Síochána. Also, we held a variety of classes, including cookery demonstrations and courses on household management. Although we never put any pressure on parents to attend, we always tried our best to cater for their needs.

The years I spent in Knocknaheeny were both challenging and exciting, especially as I was witnessing the birth and growth of a new community. Yet, as the years began to roll by, I began to realise that it was time to bring my teaching career to an end.

Since way back, I had always intended to retire from teaching at around fifty-five years of age. By the time I was fifty-seven, I felt that I was approaching a kind of a burn-out, which was not good for me and of course not good for the school. I began to think that a new person at the helm would give the school a new lease of life. So I paid a visit to my doctor and friend Séamus Looney, a dual GAA player who had won a collection of All-Ireland medals with Cork between 1967 and 1970. Without putting it in so many words, Séamus gave me the impression that it would be wise for me to end my teaching career.

Seán's last day in St Mary's on the Hill National School in July 1993.
Included are: Liz Nolan, Ger Lawton, Mary Collins, Father Liam O'Regan,
Seán, Eileen O'Leary, Colette O'Driscoll, Lorraine Downey, Father Kieran
Twomey, Deirdre O'Shea, Bernie Murphy, Patricia O'Donovan, Michelle
Healy, Pascaline Horan, Ursula Buckley, Seán Horgan, Mary McCarthy,
Margaret O'Shea, Nuala Healy, Bríd Hickey, Evelyn O'Sullivan, Noreen
Meaney, Dan O'Sullivan and Seán Ó Murchú. COURTESY GER O'DONOVAN.

When I came home, I discussed my future with Eileen and
she was in agreement that my retirement would be a good idea.
On the following morning, I resigned. Shortly afterwards,
Liz Nolan took over as principal. I was delighted when she
succeeded me. Under her direction, just as I expected, the
school got a new lease of life. She is now retired herself but she
is still remembered with love and affection by the people of
Knocknaheeny.

Vice-Principal Liz Nolan and Seán welcome (*l–r*) the late John Kerins and Tomás Mulcahy to St Mary's on the Hill National School in September 1990, the year Cork won both the football and hurling All-Ireland finals. They brought the Sam Maguire and Liam McCarthy Cups to the school after their win. COURTESY GER O'DONOVAN.

I was happy with my decision and fully embraced retirement. Now, for the first time in my life, I could concentrate more on my singing. Still, even before then, I had managed to fit in a fair share of performances. Incidentally, at this time too, for no particular reason, I decided that I would end my total abstinence and enjoy a few beers.

14

AT HOME AND ABROAD

After Seán Ó Riada died, even though we had rarely worked together in the previous few years, I felt a huge void in my singing life. Sometimes when I sang, I almost felt that he was not far away.

At the time of Seán's passing, Eileen and I had two young children; Áine, who had just turned two years of age, and Con, who was born a few weeks after Seán's death. As I wanted to be there for them as much as possible, I made up my mind that I should be totally in control of whatever singing gigs came my way. By then, my regular involvement with radio had ended, partly because I had decided to spend more time with my family.

In those days, I was in reasonable demand all over Ireland for concerts, *céilís*, cabaret, after-dinner gigs and other guest appearances. As well as singing in Ireland, I made two trips to England every year. Performing in Derby for my good Kerry friend Father Tim O'Sullivan on St Patrick's Day became an annual event. In fact, it still is.

My Derby experience has made me very aware of the wonderful work that so many Irish priests do on the English mission. Father Tim is not much younger than me and yet he seems to have the energy and commitment that enables him to work a seven-day week with many twelve-hour days included. The range of his work is enormous: the sick, the dying, the lonely and downtrodden, the bereaved are all ministered to. Then there are all the parish duties: Masses, baptisms, weddings. The list is endless. Does he relax? Yes he does: there's Kerry football and the odd game of golf. He is not too happy though when Kerry hit a bad patch, or when the putts don't sink. That's Kerry men for you!

In 1986, a young, progressive, Dublin-based recording company named Harmac Records approached me to do an album, or an LP as it was known back then. When I learned that Dónal Lunny would be the arranger and musical director of the record, I jumped at the offer. By then, Harmac Records had already recorded albums with well-known artists such as Phil Coulter, Paddy Reilly, Joe Dolan and Joseph Locke.

The method used to make the album differed greatly from the way recordings were done with Ó Riada and Ceolteóirí Chualann, whereby a recording was completed over a weekend or two successive weekends. To record for Harmac, Dónal Lunny, a group of session musicians and myself headed for Randalstown on the shores of Lough Neagh to a residential recording studio, booked by Harmac for a week and owned

In July 1986 Seán presented a CD *Heritage* to the Lord Mayor of Cork.
Back row (*l–r*): Áine, Con and Íde; front row (*l–r*): Eileen, Lord Mayor
Dan Wallace, Seán and Ethel Wallace. Photo taken by Charles Butler.

by a local man called Seán 'Mud' Wallace. Because it was a residential studio, we could work, eat and sleep in the one building and focus entirely on the job. Our group included the guitarist Des Moore, a brother of Butch. I had performed with Des on television a few times and I was delighted to see him as he was always a wonderful, sympathetic accompanist.

Making the album gave me my first experience of multi-track recording where the singer lays down the vocal track and all the other instruments are added on track by track. Dónal Lunny's command of the studio and his musicianship evident in the arrangements impressed me greatly and these arrangements that he created perfectly matched my interpretation of the songs. Some of the songs I recorded with him still rate among my favourite recordings, two in particular, 'I Know my Love' and 'Bunclody'.

While rehearsing, I was fascinated to observe Dónal transcribe each musician's line to them separately and then fuse the lot into one glorious arrangement. For me, working with him was a positive, pleasant experience. He is, of course, one of the outstanding musicians of his generation.

During the entire week, we took only one night off. All of us headed into Ballymena and treated ourselves to a Chinese meal. Although I was fifty years of age at the time, I had never indulged much in Chinese food. But, under Dónal Lunny's expert guidance on such matters, it turned out to be one of the tastiest meals I ever ate.

Later that year, I went to Salzburg to sing with the choir of the Salzburg cathedral, as part of the 1,200th anniversary of the founding of the diocese by the Irish St Fergal, who is also known as Vergilius of Salzburg. I rehearsed with the choir and orchestra under the baton of a venerable Austrian conductor, whose name escapes me.

One day, during rehearsals in the cathedral, a Cork couple, who were tourists, happened to stroll into the church. I could see them examining me as they proceeded up the nave of the huge Salzburg dome. I was singing from a pulpit and the wife stood beneath it and waited until the singing stopped. Then, in a strong Cork accent, she addressed me as follows, 'Seánó boy when I came into the church and I heard the voice I said to me husband, "It sounds like the Pucker," and when I came up the church sez I, "It looks like the Pucker," and then when I seen you up close I sez to him, "Jesus that is the Pucker." I'll go away now boy and light a candle that you'll sing good tonight.' All the poor conductor could decipher were the words 'pucker, pucker, pucker' and he confused them with a certain word beginning with 'f' which rhymes with pucker. Turning to me with a sad look on his face and in a most sympathetic tone, he said to me, 'She does not like your music, yes?'

On the day of the celebrations, Cardinal Tomás Ó Fiaich and the archbishop of Salzburg presided over the pontifical high Mass. It turned out to be a splendid occasion. A crowd of Austrian and Irish dignitaries filled the cathedral, among them the Austrian president and former secretary-general of the United Nations, Kurt Waldheim.

Later that day, a magnificent banquet was held high above the town in the glorious Hohensalzburg Castle, one of the largest medieval castles in Europe. During the meal, the woman sitting beside me told me that she had been invited because she was the granddaughter of a former archbishop of Salzburg, who obviously had not been a great admirer of celibacy.

During his stay, Cardinal Ó Fiaich visited the tiny church of St Brigid of Ireland, about 12 miles outside the city. According to local tradition, St Brigid founded the first church built on the site.

Later that evening, we all gathered in Salzburg for a singsong in a local inn. Cardinal Ó Fiaich gave a fine rendition of '*Báidín Fheilimí*' and afterwards, just as he was drinking a tankard of local beer, a press photographer arrived. Discreetly, the good cardinal passed his tankard to me. But I quickly passed it on further, out of respect for my Pioneer pin, as I was still a Pioneer at the time.

Later that year, when I was invited back to Salzburg to sing in some concerts, I decided that Eileen and our children Áine, Con and Íde should come along too. We all set off in our Ford Cortina and sailed by ferry from Rosslare to Fishguard and then drove to Dover. From there, we crossed over to Calais and drove on as far as Luxembourg. On the following day, we began a 450-mile trek to Salzburg. The journey put me to the pin of my collar, especially as I had to drive on the right-hand side of the road in narrow lanes and try to keep up with the speed of the traffic on those German *autobahns*.

By the time we reached Salzburg, darkness had already fallen. We phoned the family with whom we had arranged to stay. They came into the city and guided us to their farmhouse, high up on one of the hills above Salzburg. It was indeed fortunate that we had made that journey for the first time in darkness because when I rose the next morning and saw that we had driven on a road that ran up the side of a mountain, I wondered if I would ever have attempted the trip in daylight.

The concerts went well and Áine and Con accompanied me on the violin and accordion. We all enjoyed the trip and I suppose it's fair to say that it was our greatest family adventure.

Around that time too, I sang on various television programmes and even got my own mini series of four programmes called *An Ghaoth Aneas*. Recorded in the Muskerry Arms in Blarney, it featured Irish traditional musicians and singers.

During the 1980s also, I performed several times in *Up for the Match* television programmes, which brought viewers all the build-up to the All-Ireland finals. Those were the days when Cork made a habit of qualifying for the finals. Again, Áine and Con accompanied me when I sang on those shows and that pleased me greatly.

Also in the 1980s, RTÉ aired television programmes to commemorate Seán Ó Riada, including a set of three live shows called *The Ó Riada Retrospective*. Each programme featured a different aspect of Seán's work. I took part in the traditional night, along with a host of Irish traditional musicians, singers and dancers. For me, the person I enjoyed meeting most that night was the man I had replaced in Ceolteóirí Chualann, Darach Ó Catháin, who had come from his home in Leeds. In a way, I felt that our meeting had closed a circle. At the time, Darach's health was in decline. Sadly, he died shortly afterwards.

At the Cork Opera House, another commemoration of Seán Ó Riada featured Cór Chúil Aodha, the RTÉ Concert Orchestra and myself in a beautiful arrangement by Peadar Ó Riada of the song '*Táimse im' Chodladh*'.

I have particularly fond memories too of another concert with the orchestra around that time in a festival marquee in the grounds of University College Cork. It was a lovely, balmy June evening and a great Cork crowd turned up and joined heartily in the singing of 'De Banks'.

Since my early days of performing, radio has been my favourite medium, maybe because doing a radio programme is not as demanding as appearing on television. Also, radio often produces a more satisfying result as well as a higher standard of performance in a much more intimate setting.

Through working on radio, I came to admire many of its presenters, among them my good friend Donncha Ó Dulaing, the voice of rural Ireland, whom I met for the first time when I performed on his radio programme *Munster Journal.* Donncha understands his audience well and connects with them in great style. Their love for him is exceeded only by the devotion of all the Irish-born reverend mothers and nuns in convents throughout the United Kingdom. Over the years, he recorded a series of memorable programmes, such as those on holy wells, his walks around Ireland, his tour of the country with the relics of St Therese and *Fáilte Isteach*. And, of course, he has given stirring accounts of Munster finals. No doubt

Seán and good friend and accompanist Dan Coakley at the Parish Hall, Glengarriff, County Cork, December 1986 at the start of a Beara to Breffini walk by Donncha Ó Dúlaing.

the wonderful series of interviews he recorded with President Éamon de Valera will provide valuable information for history students in the years ahead. One would hope that he would go on forever.

133

Also, through working in radio, I came across another great interviewer, Colm Keane from Youghal. Regardless of who he is interviewing, Colm can draw out every bit of information on any subject.

Another performer I admired was Joe Lynch, who first shot to fame in the 1950s with his radio show *Living with Lynch* and later became a well-known actor. He will forever be remembered for his wonderful portrayal of Dinny Byrne in the popular television series *Glenroe.* Joe and I performed together in concerts in England, including two shows in the Royal Albert Hall. Shortly after the Birmingham bombing of 1974, we performed together at the Digbeth Hall in Birmingham. It was a tense night, with a security presence of about 180 policemen in the hall and its vicinity. We were told that each and every one of them was of Irish descent.

As well as working with Radio Éireann on programmes such as *Céilí House,* I did a good deal of work too with Raidió na Gaeltachta, a station that has done great work for the preservation of the Irish language and culture. The station has a wealth of fine broadcasters. I've had the pleasure of being interviewed by many of them, including Jeaic Ó Muircheartaigh, Helen Ní Shé and Pádraig Ó Sé and my favourite footballer of all time, *fear uasal,* a gentleman to his finger-tips, Dara Ó Cinnéide. For four years, I served on the advisory board of Raidió na Gaeltachta and that gave me a wonderful insight into the toil and dedication of all who work there and the sacrifices they make to ensure that the station serves the purpose for which it was founded. To me, Raidió na

Seán sings with the RTÉ Concert Orchestra, conducted by Proinnsias
Ó Duinn, in June 1999 at the opening of the Cork Arts Festival.
COURTESY *IRISH EXAMINER.*

Gaeltachta is without a doubt the most important station, be it radio or television, operating in this country at present.

Way back in the early 1960s, I had often performed with the Blarney Céilí Band at *céilís* in Cashel in Halla na Féile for an organisation called Cumann an Phiarsaigh, which was dedicated to the promotion of Irish culture. It was headed up by a young man from Cashel named Labhrás Ó Murchú. Later, he became the Director General of Comhaltas Ceoltóirí Éireann – an organisation founded in 1951 to promote Irish traditional music, song and dance as well as the Irish language. What Labhrás did for Comhaltas Ceoltóirí Éireann is similar to what Pádraig Ó Caoimh did for the GAA. Pádraig took the GAA by the scruff of the neck, laid down the structures and systems and wielded it into a vibrant community-based national organisation. Likewise, Labhrás developed Comhaltas into the mighty force it is today, with over 400 branches worldwide.

For much of my life, although I had always been a member of Comhaltas, I had rarely been active in the organisation, as teaching came first and singing took up the rest of my spare time. However, in 2005, Labhrás rang me and asked if I would be interested in going to America as a presenter and singer in a Comhaltas tour of America called Echoes of Erin. I had no hesitation whatsoever in accepting his offer.

The ten-day trip was a totally new experience for me. We toured the southern states and performed in places such as Cocoa Beach, Florida; Panama City, Oklahoma; and Saint Louis, Missouri. By Ireland's standards, the distance between

Seán receives a Millennium Award from Lord Mayor Damian Wallace
in March 2000 for his contribution to education and culture in Cork.
Courtesy Mike English.

each venue was vast. Often, we covered 400 miles in one day
by bus. One morning, as we were driving to yet another venue,
our bus broke down, which added even more to the excitement
of the tour.

During the trip, and indeed on subsequent Comhaltas tours, I found that the camaraderie and good humour of the group always deflated any tensions that arose on the long-distance journeys. On that first tour, I became great friends with Martin Donohoe, the marvellous, flamboyant Cavan accordionist who can walk on stage and have the audience in the palm of his hand even before he plays his first note. In later years, Martin and I toured together a lot. Even today, I often drive to Cavan to perform with him and he sometimes comes to Cork to do gigs with me.

Also, on that first Comhaltas tour, I met the renowned Wexford *uilleann* piper Pádraig Sinnott for the first time. A master of his instrument, he played a huge range of reels, jigs and hornpipes. I admired him greatly, especially for his rendering of slow airs. Pádraig had a deep interest in the history of his county, particularly in the 1798 rebellion. Once, I went with him to Vinegar Hill, where British troops defeated the Wexford rebels. There, he recalled with passion the story of the 1978 rising. To hear him playing 'Boolavogue' and 'The Croppy Boy' and to realise what he is thinking of as he does so is a unique and moving experience.

Around 2008, I headed to Canada with Comhaltas. We played in a French-speaking area near Montreal known as Shannon and called after the Shannon River. The small, compact community, led by a wonderful organiser named Maureen Maher, put in great preparation for our visit and hung a beautiful backdrop of an Irish rural scene in the hall

Seán at the Kremlin, Moscow, in November 2009.

where we performed. The audience there was one of the best I have come across.

On the following night, we performed in Montreal in an even bigger hall, with Maureen Maher involved once again. Although the audience were great, they did not have the sharpness of the people in Shannon.

On the following day, we drove north to Saskatoon, the largest city in the prairie province of Saskatchewan. We stayed with the family of Kieran Brennan. A well-known sportsman,

Kieran had played football with Down in the 1980s and had been a member of the team that went on to win the Sam Maguire in 1991, but he left for Canada before the final to take up a teaching post in Saskatoon.

The weather changed overnight in Saskatoon. On the day we arrived, I was strolling in the sunshine, while the next day we had three-quarters of an inch of snow. Winter had begun and the snow was expected to stay for four months. Although the snow came suddenly, road workers managed to clear it away, as they were well equipped with snow ploughs, and life went on as normal.

Of all the places we visited in Canada, perhaps our trip to Manitou, which is a tiny village at a crossroad in the district of Manitoba, was the most interesting. The Manitoba Opera House seated about two hundred and was crammed to the rafters for our performance. A pig farmer with over a thousand sows had organised the show. He had a huge interest in Irish traditional music, even though he had no connection whatsoever with Ireland. Many of our group stayed in his house. They found it hard going, putting up with the aroma of the pigs all night. But the rashers the following morning were divine.

We also visited Ottawa, which had a good, vibrant branch of Comhaltas. Our performance took place in the beautiful, municipal town hall building. We had an audience of about four hundred, but the huge hall was more than half empty. For two nights, we stopped off in Winnipeg, a most unusual city, divided into two by the river. On one side, the population spoke only English and those on the other side spoke only French.

From Winnipeg we moved on to Detroit, the most populous city in the state of Michigan, now ravaged by the decline of the auto industry. To me the city was a kind of a desolate urban jungle. We had a meal in a nice restaurant called the Cork Tavern. The local organisation of Comhaltas warned us not to stray too far from the restaurant and not to wander off on our own.

When we went along to the concert venue, we were amazed to see that 'Conradh na Gaeilge Detroit' was written over the door. As I waited outside for some others to come along, a big, burly American approached me. He stopped, looked at me and asked, 'Do you come from Ireland? Are you here with the group? Are you a singer?' Then, to my surprise, he said, 'Did you sing with the great Seán Ó Riada? Is your name Ó Sé?' When I told him that I was the very man, he bellowed in a loud American drawl, 'God almighty man, I thought you passed away years ago!' That remark rather deflated my ego!

As well as touring Canada with Comhaltas, I went with them to Moscow in November 2010. Our group included: Ireland's then piping champion Martino Vacca from Italy; all-Ireland champion dancer and multi-instrumentalist Tara Breen from Clare; all-Ireland accordion champion Pádraig King; our leader, flute player Siobhán Ní Chonaráin; and dancer and concertina player Gearóid Keane from Naas, who must have got his flair for the concertina from his famous uncle Noel Hill.

The tour was organised by an Irish-speaking Russian musician named Yuri Andreichuk, who looked like Lenin and was the leader of about forty Russians, all of whom had adopted an Irish lifestyle. They spoke Irish, played Irish music, held *céilís* and set up a branch of Comhaltas Ceoltóirí Éireann.

It seemed strange that I should be heading to Moscow, especially as I was supposed to go there back in the 1960s with Seán Ó Riada and Ceoltóirí Chualann to play a few concerts. That trip had been arranged by Mick O'Riordan, a Cork man known to all as Red Mick. He was the leader of the Irish Communist Party and had a great *grá* for Irish music. Mick sent the *Ó Riada sa Gaiety* album and other Ó Riada albums to Moscow and they became popular on Radio Moscow. An invitation to perform in Russia followed. However, some months before we were due to fly out, a political reform movement called the Prague Spring staged an uprising in Czechoslovakia. The Soviet Union mercilessly crushed the rebels and that put an end to our tour. Now here I was, more than forty years later, setting off for Russia with Comhaltas Ceoltóirí Éireann.

We landed in Domodedova Airport on the outskirts of Moscow and headed by train to the city centre. When we stepped off the train, Yuri was there to greet us. He welcomed us to Moscow in Irish, '*Céad míle fáilte go cathair Moscow, príomh chathair na Rúise.*' From the train station, we went by taxi to our hotel, a journey that took three hours to complete, as heavy traffic in Moscow that evening brought the city to a complete standstill.

On the next day, we toured the walled Kremlin complex in the heart of Moscow, which serves as the official residence of Russia's president and boasts five palaces, four cathedrals and towers. We stood in awe in front of Lenin's Tomb in Red Square, where his embalmed body has been on display since 1924. We stopped too on the spot where Stalin reviewed his troops as they marched by during parades and commemorations and we marvelled at the beauty of St Basil's Cathedral, with its many domes shaped as the flames of a bonfire rising high into the sky.

For most of the following day, we rehearsed. That evening, when we turned up for the actual concert at the stage door of the theatre, the Central House of Artists, an elderly man with a wispy beard stepped forward, clutching an album by Seán Ó Riada entitled *Ceol na nUasal*. He told us that he was one of the men who had organised the aborted tour back in the 1960s. He became highly emotional and indeed so did I.

The concert was a huge success. For my first song, I sang 'Sliabh na mBan'. I don't think that I ever got such a sustained applause for any one song. It was one of those occasions when I felt in an almost tangible fashion the presence of Seán Ó Riada. It's at times like these too that I always regret so bitterly that he was taken at such an early age.

During the rest of our stay, a great Dublin character of Kerry parentage named Diarmuid Fleming gave us a tour of Moscow. At the time, he was working there as a journalist. He brought us to clubs and venues in Moscow, all of which led me to the conclusion that there is a side to Moscow that is similar to other big cities.

Without a doubt, the best way to travel in Moscow is by underground train. Yet, I always found it intimidating and scary.

One memorable night in Sally O'Brien's pub in Moscow, some high-ranking, classical musicians from Moscow's famous orchestras turned up to relax by playing Irish jigs, reels and hornpipes. In particular, I recall a duet of Irish reels played by Tara Breen and the deputy leader of one such orchestra.

In 2010 on the banks of the Huangpu River, Shanghai staged World Expo 2010, China's first world fair and the biggest in history, with the largest number of countries taking part and a site of over 5.28 square kilometres. It ran from 1 May to 31 October. Along with other Comhaltas Ceoltóirí musicians from Brú Ború in Cashel, I was invited to visit and perform there for a period of ten days, to coincide with the visit of President Mary McAleese and her husband, Martin.

Each day, we performed twice at the Irish Pavilion. It proved to be one of the most popular exhibits of the trade fair and attracted a constant stream of visitors. The focal part of our stay was the arrival of President McAleese.

While in Shanghai, the president and her party stayed at the Mandarin Hotel. The highlight of President McAleese's visit was a state banquet she hosted in the Mandarin for Chinese business people and Irish people working in Shanghai, many of whom were doing extremely well at the head of various enterprises. Some well-known Irish people came over especially for the fair and banquet, among them the famous Cavan chef Neven Maguire.

On the whole, I found that the Chinese authorities were extremely security conscious, especially on the night of the banquet, at which we had been invited to perform. Prior to the banquet, the authorities locked down the hotel and ushered us all into a big room as a complete security sweep got underway in the rest of the building. Before we were allowed to leave the room, we underwent the strictest security check I have ever experienced. In all my life, I never felt as safe as I did that night in Shanghai.

Ever since Mary McAleese became president of Ireland in 1997, I have admired her. But my high regard for her increased even further when I saw at first-hand in Shanghai her work rate, energy and dedication to her role, as well as the pride and love she showed for the country she represented. After our performance, she met us as a group and spent much time chatting to each of us. Early on the following morning, we made our way to an auditorium in the centre of Shanghai, where 400 Chinese women had gathered to hear a speech by President McAleese. There she was before us again, bright and early, fresh as a daisy, and ready and eager to start yet another busy day.

Overall, I found that Shanghai was a city of contrasts. Whenever I visit a foreign city, I always love to explore it and walk around on my own. Although I didn't wander too far away from our hotel, I did stroll into a smart area of lovely shops, boutiques and restaurants. However, when I walked only a short distance in the opposite direction, I found myself in the midst of terrible poverty and run-down streets, with horrible odours all around. The restaurants there fascinated me. Outside each restaurant stood a huge tank full of monstrous eels, swimming and splashing about. Chinese people showed great interest in the tanks and chatted excitedly as they picked out their own eels.

During our stay, I learned that Chinese food as we know it is not at all like the food that the Chinese actually eat. One night, at a banquet in our hotel, when a huge plate of whole fish was put in front of us, the Chinese scrambled to select the best fish and the first parts of the fish they ate were the eyes, which they seemed to regard as a special delicacy.

After ten days or more, it was time to bid farewell to Shanghai. Although I enjoyed my time there, I was glad to go home.

By the end of World Expo 2010, 73 million people had visited the exhibition and 246 countries had taken part. In the history of the world's fairs, it was the most expensive Expo of all.

When I came home from Shanghai, I continued performing with the group of traditional musicians, singers and dancers called Brú Ború. The group is resident in a heritage centre also known as Brú Ború. Founded at the foot of the Rock of Cashel by Úna Ó Murchú, the wife of Senator Labhrás Ó Murchú, director general of Comhaltas, the centre includes a theatre, a restaurant, a fine craft shop, bar facilities, conference rooms, part of the Comhaltas Archive and quite a unique and spectacular cultural exhibition entitled *Sounds of History*, which recalls the story of Ireland from ancient times to the present day.

As well as performing in shows in the Brú Ború theatre for five nights each week during the summer months, right up until late August, the group also performs at various venues around the country.

When Úna Ó Murchú invited me to sing with Brú Ború, I was absolutely delighted and felt honoured to have been chosen. Even to this day, I still frequently perform with them and have travelled with the group to faraway places, such as Parsippany in New Jersey.

Since its foundation, Brú Ború has gone from strength to strength. Úna deserves much credit for its success. She has brought together the best traditional musicians, singers and dancers from Cashel and further afield and has made them one of the most cohesive and entertaining groups performing Irish traditional music today. They regularly perform at conferences, festivals and gatherings all over Ireland and abroad. During Ireland's last presidency of the European Union, Brú Ború performed for nearly all the visiting delegations and dignitaries.

Over the years, I've made many foreign trips with my good friend Matthew Allen, whom I met quite by chance. One day, a good few years ago now, as I was chatting to a friend of mine near Patrick's Bridge in Cork, I became aware of a tall, bearded gentleman standing nearby, staring intently at me. When my friend moved on, he approached me and introduced himself as Matthew Allen, an ethnomusicologist who taught at

Wheaton College, a university of the arts near Boston. I was impressed when he told me he recognised me from the timbre of my voice, which he heard on one of my recordings. He was interested in hearing me sing in the flesh and wondered if I had any local gigs coming up. I told him I was singing in Dungarvan that very night and invited him to come along. He did and so began an enduring friendship.

We have had some great nights together at all kinds of gigs. He accompanied me on guitar and piano in both Ireland and America. We made some television programmes together and over a period of a few years he filmed, edited and produced an hour-long documentary on my life and times, which can be viewed on the Vimeo website. He invited me twice to Wheaton College as a visiting scholar to work with some of his own and his wife Julie's students and to sing at a few concerts in Boston. I asked him to come with me to the Boston Beara Society dinner. We had a great time at that event.

Recently, he brought me on one of the most interesting trips I ever made. We travelled to The Celtic Colours Festival on the island of Cape Breton, which is off the northeastern coast of Nova Scotia and is actually connected to the mainland by a long causeway. I flew from Cork to Heathrow and directly from there to Halifax and then on to the town of Sydney on the northeastern tip of Cape Breton. There was music everywhere and the fiddle is king in this part of the world. Indeed, on the pier in Stanley is a statue of a fiddle about 10 metres in height. We toured around the island and we were fortunate that it

Seán entertains senior citizens in Mallow, County Cork, in May 2010.

was the time of year when the woods were resplendent in the colours of autumn.

Everywhere we stopped on our trip there were groups of musicians, mostly fiddlers, playing away. The traditional style has been well preserved in Cape Breton and *céilís* have become a popular attraction. Some performers have received significant recognition outside of Cape Breton, including people like

Bruce Guthro, Buddy MacMaster, Natalie MacMaster, the Rankin Family and the Barra MacNeils. At the festival, we heard a wonderful array of visiting musicians from Mali, the Ukraine, the Czech Republic, Poland and, of course, Scotland. One of the most popular performers was the well-known Irish *sean-nós* singer Lillis Ó Laoire.

Everything was good about Cape Breton. The scenery was wonderful, as was the weather, although we were told we were lucky with that aspect. The people were extremely welcoming and friendly and, as for food, I don't think I ever ate as much lobster in my life. We were sad to be leaving but, as I said before, there's no place like home. The Irish proverb, '*Níl aon tinteán mar do thinteán féin*' – there's no fireside like your own fireside – comes to mind.

In early 2011, another long-distance tour with Comhaltas beckoned. A group of us flew to Cuba, the largest island in the Caribbean with a population of over 11 million. Once again, Siobhán Ní Chonaráin took on the role of leader and we were joined by the celebrated fiddler Eileen O'Brien from Nenagh.

Without a doubt, Cuba is a strange country. The Americans made it extremely difficult for anyone to travel to the island, while the Cuban communist revolutionary and politician Fidel Castro made it hard for anyone to leave.

When we arrived in Cuba, officials did not stamp our passports. Instead, they inserted a stamped page, which they took out again when we were leaving the country. Later, I learned the reason for this is that anyone with a passport stamped in Cuba cannot gain entry into the United States.

Seán, MC, at the 2011 Fleadh Cheoil na Mumhan in the Oriel House, Ballincollig, County Cork. COURTESY *IRISH EXAMINER*.

During our stay, we based ourselves in the older part of Cuba's capital city, Havana, a major port and leading commercial centre. In all my travels, I have never seen a city like it, or, more precisely, a city of such unique atmosphere. First of all, I noticed the extraordinary amount of licensed premises. Most of them had restaurants attached and each one had a resident band. The music was lively and full of rhythm, while all of the musicians had big smiles on their faces and seemed to be thoroughly enjoying themselves. In total contrast to all of that, only a couple of yards away, groups of men lay on the streets, almost one on top of the other, not drunk in any way, but seemingly overcome by the extreme heat and humidity. Each man seemed to be accompanied by a large dog, usually lying in a semi-comatose state on the street and also overcome, it seemed, by the same extreme heat and humidity. Everywhere, people sold cigars, which they claimed were Cuba's best-selling cigars. It seemed unlikely, but as none of us smoked, we couldn't dispute that claim.

One morning, when I went for a stroll, I came across a huge queue of people outside a state-controlled bakery, where each person seemed to collect about a half loaf of bread, which may have been their daily ration of food. The streets were filthy and many had open sewers.

In another part of the city stands the parliamentary building. Architecturally, it's almost a clone of the Capitol building in Washington. Only a street away, I saw the worst slums I have ever seen in my travels. From many of the windows, gaunt and hungry-looking women stared out aimlessly at passers-by.

Yet, nearby, I saw an opulent, five-star hotel built for foreign dignitaries and wealthy tourists. It claimed that its ice cream cocktails were world-famous. Having sampled one, I can vouch for the claim; indeed, I went back for a few more.

In Havana, almost every car on the road was a vintage American Cadillac or Ford petrol guzzler. Most of them were run-down and badly kept.

Our hotel, Hotel Ambos Mundos, proved interesting. It was clean and functional and according to Cuban standards had a three-star rating. In Ireland, it would probably fail to be even classified as a hotel. Its claim to fame was that Ernest Hemingway had written one of his novels while staying there. As a result, every bus tour of Havana stopped at the hotel and groups of tourists, mostly French, went inside to have a look at his room.

Our concert was held in the National Theatre of Cuba. A shabby and run-down venue, most of the material on the arms of the seats had disappeared, while many of the seats could not be put into position. Backstage was even worse. Between the green room and the stage lay an open sewer, around which all performers had to pass to make their way to the stage. Yet, despite all of that, our concerts went down well and we felt that our journey had been worthwhile.

I was delighted to learn recently that the United States, acting on the initiative of President Obama, has lifted the embargo on travel to and from Cuba. Let us all hope that this signals better times ahead for Cuba and particularly its people, who richly deserve a better quality of life.

15

THE SIGHTSEERS

After I retired from teaching in 1993 at the age of fifty-seven, Eileen and I decided to make the most of our good health and free time and see some of the world. Until then, we had rarely been abroad together during our married life. While the children were young, we rarely holidayed outside Ireland. Apart from our memorable trip to Salzburg, we ventured no further afield than England. So we decided to make up a little for lost time.

Immediately after I retired, we headed for Scotland and retraced our honeymoon steps. We based ourselves in the small, resort town of Oban on the west coast and travelled all around from there. We sailed out to the Isle of Mull, the second largest island of the Inner Hebrides, and also visited the nearby island of Iona, where Colmcille founded a monastery which served as a centre of Irish monasticism for four centuries. One night, we attended a concert in the local town hall, where Jimmy Shand

and his Band topped the bill and where we saw a wonderful display of Scottish highland dancing. On the whole, Scottish music, and indeed Scottish dancing too, is a little more sedate than the Irish versions. Nevertheless, we enjoyed the concert to no end.

As well as indulging in some entertainment, we made a trip to St Margaret's Church in Lochgilphead in Argyll, where the famous Scottish tenor Canon Sydney MacEwan had served as parish priest for seventeen years. There, we admired the beautiful stained glass window dedicated to his family. Ever since I can remember, I have loved Canon MacEwan's recording of 'Bring Flowers of the Rarest'. Each year, to mark the first day of May, Gay Byrne kept up a lovely tradition of playing it on his radio programme *The Gay Byrne Hour*, a custom now continued by Ronan Collins on *The Ronan Collins Show*.

After our trip to Scotland, we turned our eyes to Europe and ventured first of all to Paris, where we did all the usual tours. We visited the Palace of Versailles, treated ourselves to a performance by the Paris Opera Ballet and took on the more strenuous task of climbing to the summit of Montmartre to see the white-domed Basilica of the Sacré Coeur, from where we gazed down on the beauty of Paris. Since our first trip to the City of Light, we returned many times to explore even further. Every time we go back, we discover something new.

Next, we flew to Rome. When we attended Mass celebrated by Pope John Paul ll in St Peter's Square, the pope was so far away that we could barely see him. But at least we can claim that we were there.

During the following year, we went to Prague, Budapest and Vienna. We were captivated by each city's rich store of history, their palaces and churches and the scenery in all three. Prague has The Charles Bridge, Prague Castle, St Vitus Cathedral and its Old Town. Budapest comprises the twin cities of Buda and Pest, linked by the famous Chain Bridge across the River Danube, with beautiful parliament buildings lining the river bank. Vienna, also on the Danube, has the Schonbrunn Palace close by and in the city centre stands St Stephen's Cathedral with its remarkable roof.

Of all the cities we visited, we enjoyed Munich the most. The city had a vibrancy all of its own. The weather was fine and we spent many nights in the Hofbrauhaus am Platzl, a huge beer hall in the city centre, where we listened to a wonderful, rousing German beer-tent band and we sampled a few tankards of German beer.

During our stay, we visited the Dachau concentration camp, which was the first concentration camp opened by the Nazis and now stands as a memorial to all the Jewish people who were incinerated there. It is a frightening reminder of the unimaginable evil of Hitler and Nazi Germany. We saw many reminders of the horrific conditions in these concentration camps but I will never forget the preserved ovens where thousands met their fate. Even after leaving, I still thought I could smell the stench of burning flesh. It seems hard to imagine that such evil might be repeated anywhere. Yet, only twenty years ago we had the Rwanda Genocide.

On another trip to Germany, we went to Berlin. By then, the city was unified. Yet, plenty of signs remained of the divisions created in the city after the defeat of the Germans in the Second World War. We saw Checkpoint Charlie, a name given by the Western Allies to the best-known Berlin Wall crossing point between East Berlin and West Berlin during the Cold War. Today, it has become a popular, light-hearted tourist attraction. But more sombre reminders of a troubled past remain, including a small section of the Berlin Wall. Also, we visited an area where rebel Germans were tortured and murdered by Hitler's henchmen. When we entered the former East Berlin, we noticed a much different atmosphere, emphasised all the more by drab and dreary buildings of the Communist regime. Close to our hotel, we saw the Kaiser Wilhelm Memorial Church, which was badly damaged in a bombing raid in 1943. Now, the remains of its spire stand as a stark reminder of the evils of war and of man's inhumanity to man.

In our travels, we ventured to Poland too and explored the picturesque and historical city of Krakow. Although devastated during the Second World War, the city has been restored to its former glory, literally stone by stone. We spent a few days there, strolling through its streets of colourful buildings and dining each evening in its fine restaurants.

In Warsaw, we stayed in the eighty-two-storey Marriott Hotel, from which we could see many other equally tall hotels, such as the Novotel Warsaw Centrum Hotel, the Westin and the Sofitel. All the well-known American hotel chains seemed to be represented. In the midst of these stood a huge, grey building, built by the Soviet Union as its centre of administration. Today, local opinion is divided about whether it should be preserved as a reminder of the Communist era or demolished to signify the end of Polish oppression. So far, those who believe the building should be retained seem to have won the argument.

Every summer since my retirement, Eileen and I make an annual trip to London, along with my sister Maureen, who is also happily retired. While Eileen and Maureen satisfy their thirst for the theatre, I usually find some jazz clubs, preferably those featuring traditional Dixieland jazz.

In 1995, like Christopher Columbus, Eileen and I turned our eyes to the New World and flew out by our national airline to John F. Kennedy International Airport. My cousins Eileen Reynolds and her brother Paddy O'Sullivan, both from Adrigole, collected us, entertained us at their home and later dropped us off at our hotel, the Lexington on 48th Street, in the centre of Manhattan.

During our four-day stay, we took a memorable boat trip all around the island of Manhattan and got a bird's-eye view of the entire city. Later, we visited the Statue of Liberty on Ellis Island, the gateway for millions of immigrants to the United States. Its museum gave us a great insight into the trials and tribulations of Irish emigrants as they struggled to find a new life away from Ireland. Eileen found the trip particularly poignant, as her father, a Kerry man, Denis Tangney from Kilcummin near Killarney, had emigrated to America at the age of twenty-three and of course she visualised him queuing up for inspection. As we searched through the records, we found out that he had sailed there on the *Saint Francis,* that his brother Nicholas, a fireman in New York, had sponsored him, that he had £50 in his pocket when he left Ireland and that he was free of any disease that would prevent him entering the country. Eileen recalled that he worked hard in New York for nine years and saved enough money to buy a farm near Killeagh in east Cork, where she was born.

One night, Judy O'Sullivan, another cousin of mine, took us up after night-fall to the viewing balcony of the Twin Towers. In particular, I remember the sight of helicopters far down below us, circling around the city, bringing groups on night-time trips over New York. Those towers, of course, were demolished in the 9/11 attack.

From New York, we took a short flight to Washington. We visited the meeting place of the United States Congress, and Senate on Capitol Hill, and were surprised that we were able to gain entry to both without delay or difficulty. We had lunch in the Dirksen Senate Office Building and later viewed the Lincoln Memorial and the Korean War Veterans' Memorial in West Potomac Park.

For both of us, the saddest place we visited on our trip to Washington was the Vietnam Veterans' Memorial, erected to honour service members of the US armed forces who fought in the Vietnam War, service members who died in service in Vietnam and South East Asia and service members who were unaccounted for during the war. It consists of three separate sections: the Three Soldiers' Statue; the Vietnam Women's

Memorial; and the Vietnam Veterans' Memorial Wall, which bears 58,195 names, all inscribed in alphabetical order. While standing at the memorial, we saw a group of Vietnam veterans from a veterans' home in North Carolina. As they gazed at the memorial, they sobbed uncontrollably for a fallen comrade whose name was engraved on the wall.

We visited Boston too. In comparison to New York and Washington, it had a more European feel about it, with many visible signs of Irish influence. We walked the Boston Freedom Trail; a red-brick pathway that runs for 2.5 miles and links together significant local landmarks. At Harvard, we toured the John F. Kennedy Presidential Library and Museum. It houses original papers and correspondence of the Kennedy Administration, as well as special collections of published and unpublished material, including books and papers by and about Ernest Hemingway. Near the end of the tour, we strolled into a room dedicated to the president's visit to Ireland, where we watched a video of his departure from Shannon. Much to my amazement, the music accompanying the video featured me singing 'The Shores of Amerikay', which I had recorded with Seán Ó Riada for a film called *Kennedy's Ireland*. Following the assassination of the president, the film was never released.

As we made our way towards the exit of the building, Eileen and I couldn't resist the temptation of telling the story to the receptionist. As it happened, she hailed from Galway. On hearing our tale, she made a big fuss of us and took us up to the top storey of the building to the private room reserved for the Kennedy family. We were happy to see that all the scrolls and awards President Kennedy received on his visit to Ireland were displayed there. In one of the places of honour, we saw the beautiful, silver scroll that Cork Corporation presented to the president at City Hall in Cork on 28 June 1963 when he was awarded the Freedom of Cork. Both Eileen and I were left with the clear impression that the Kennedys truly valued their Irish roots.

On 11 September 2001, while I was doing some gardening at home, Eileen called me and told me of the horrific terrorist attacks that had taken place in New York and Washington DC. We spent the entire day glued to the television, watching the terrible tragedy unfold.

At the time, we had received an invitation to the wedding of Eileen's niece and god-daughter Angela Moloney, which was due to take place about a month later in Santa Barbara, not too far from San Francisco.

Before the wedding, we visited San Diego, where we viewed a fleet of large US Navy warships berthed there. Locals told us that these ships are in a state of constant readiness for deployment to any part of the world should the need arise. We also went on a day trip across the Mexican Border to visit the town of Tijuana, home of Herb Alpert and his renowned band The Tijuana Brass. We found the poverty there disturbing and were shocked to see an open-air meat market with no hygiene whatsoever. On our way back up to Santiago, we saw Mexicans running along the road, trying to escape over the border, hoping for a better life in the States.

We also stayed in the beautiful and extraordinary city of San Francisco. Every morning, we went to the beach to see the fog being burned off and the sun emerge. We took a bus tour across the Golden Gate Bridge and went up to Napa Valley, known as one of the world's leading wine regions. Along the way, we stopped at a few of the vineyards, including one called The Christian Brothers' Winery. Each night during our stay we dined in one of the many lovely and very reasonably priced restaurants in the city's famed Fisherman's Wharf.

After touring San Francisco, we headed for Las Vegas. There, we strolled along the 3-mile Las Vegas Strip, with its mass of casinos and entertainment centres. The whole economy of Las Vegas is based on the gambling industry. Ninety-eight per cent of the money spent on gambling is returned in prizes. However, the gross income is so large that the 2 per cent left is sufficient to pay for the upkeep and services provided by the city, which means that the city's residents have no municipal taxes to pay.

We toured the city and went into some of its casinos. We stayed at the western end of the strip, in the Hilton Hotel, where Elvis had performed when he did his stint in Las Vegas. One night, we went to a musical in the hotel's cabaret lounge called *Starlight Express*. The special effects were stunning. The hotel's buffet breakfast was the best breakfast I have ever come across, with a huge selection in everything and about eight options in eggs, all cooked to order. Although Macroom Oatmeal was not on the menu and I missed that.

In New Orleans, we stayed near the French Quarter. Our hotel gave a wonderful view of the levees that protected the city from floods. At one end of Bourbon Street – the most famous street in the French Quarter – musicians played Cajun music, which is a fusion of French and Irish music from Newfoundland and Nova Scotia. At the other end, some unbelievable bands played traditional Dixieland jazz at a variety of venues, among them the Preservation Hall, where veteran jazz musicians perform nightly. Every time we went there, it was packed, with some of the patrons sitting on the timber floor. All the musicians were legends in their own right and played mostly jazz standards, finishing each night with 'The Saints'.

On 10 October 2001, exactly four weeks after the terrorist attacks, we flew into New York on our way back home from the wedding. The city was still in shock. Before 9/11, one of the most identifiable traits of the city had been the way motorists constantly hooted their horns at one another. Now, as we travelled by taxi through the streets of the city, there was a weird silence. Any time an ambulance sounded its alarm, the whole street went into shock and people stopped talking. Every church we visited, including St Patrick's Cathedral, was packed with people praying on bended knees.

We stayed in the Lexington and walked down to see what was left of the Twin Towers. We stood within 400 yards of it and saw an ambulance speeding out of the site, perhaps with the remains of yet another of the deceased. The stench in the area was extraordinary. We were told it was the scent of burned flesh. Although I was absolutely horrified at the attacks, I was also saddened to think that Americans never took into account the number of people killed in Iraq under the rule of George W. Bush.

All in all, Eileen and I thoroughly enjoyed our many trips abroad. Life was good for us both and our children too were healthy and happy. By now, Áine was lecturing in maths in the Cork Institute of Technology and enjoying gigging with her violin in her spare time. Con, who worked as an engineer with Bord Gáis, had married Caitríona Forbes from Cloghroe in County Cork and by then had three children, Méabh, Seán and Ciara. Our youngest daughter Íde was and still is a secondary school teacher in Drogheda.

But, as we were soon to find out, life for me was about to change.

16

A Battle with Cancer

After coming home from my trip to Cuba with Comhaltas, I felt a little under the weather. On second thoughts, I feel that is putting it a little too mildly. I felt very much under the weather. I had a constant nagging ache in my stomach and I was totally lacking in energy. At first, I took little notice as I thought I might have contacted a virus while in Cuba, something a few of the group had complained of when we returned. Finally, a week or two later, when I saw no signs of improvement, indeed the reverse was the case, I made up my mind to pay a visit to our local doctor Séamus Looney.

For many years, Séamus has been my doctor and has always looked after me well. I have complete faith in him, which is very valuable to somebody like me, a bit of a hypochondriac. And here am I within striking distance of eighty. In the 1970s, Séamus was a well-known hurler and won a few All-Ireland medals with Cork. He was one of that rare breed of GAA dual players, men who represented their county in both hurling and football.

To get back to my story, when I stepped inside his surgery, I felt him looking intensely at me. He told me that he didn't like my pallor and suggested some blood tests. The results prompted further investigation and a colonoscopy revealed that I had a tumour in my colon, which was quickly diagnosed as being malignant. In other words, I had cancer.

Like many people, I had often thought about how I might cope if ever I got cancer. Indeed, I had convinced myself that I would not be very good at dealing with the disease. However, strange as it may seem, once I was diagnosed I felt as if the enemy had been identified and that there was a battle to be fought, and hopefully won, between me and the cancer. It was almost a relief to know what was wrong with me. I also felt encouraged by a friend of mine and indeed by Séamus Looney, who both said that if you were given a choice of where you might have cancer that the colon was about the best place to get it as the survival rate was good. Their assurances eased my worries and kept up my morale.

In only a matter of days, I found myself as a patient at the Bon Secours Hospital in Cork. Initially, I was put under the care of Dr Eoin O'Sullivan. When he visited me, he reminded me of Pádraig O'Sullivan, who had been at Coláiste Íosagáin and St Pat's with me. Of course, I had to tell him this and it turned out that I was right – he was his son. I felt that was indeed a good omen.

Soon, a date was set for my operation and the surgeon Mr Colm O'Boyle called to see me. I got the impression that he was confident that he could operate by using keyhole surgery, which would mean that the operation itself would be relatively minor and that I might be home in a little over a week. Later, I met the oncologist Dr Brian Bird. He spoke to me first in Irish and told me that he was a great admirer of the music of Seán Ó Riada. Another good omen said I to myself! If hurling breeds good GPs, surely an appreciation of Ó Riada's music must be of benefit to any oncologist.

The night before the operation was a time for reflection, to look back over my life. Up until then, the only time I'd had an anaesthetic was when I was ten years of age and had my tonsils removed. Deep down, I suppose I was fearful of the operation. I can clearly recall getting the notion that I might not survive it. So, in my own way, I had a chat with the Lord and, being only too aware of my shortcomings and failings, I prayed to Him that He might find a corner for me somewhere in paradise if the worst happened.

It was fairly late in the evening of the following day by the time I made it to the operating theatre. When I woke up after the operation, a nurse was standing at my side. With a big smile on her face, she said to me, 'I am Martina Warren's sister.' Martina is a good friend of mine who taught with me in Knocknaheeny. The good omens were coming fast and furious. Soon, Mr O'Boyle came along. He shook my hand and said, 'We are where we want to be.'

I stayed in the hospital for four days and they were happy days, as it seemed that the operation had been a success, the cancer had not spread and the prognosis was good. Many visitors called and wished me well and every visitor boosted my morale a little more.

On the morning I returned home, a function was taking place to mark the retirement of my good friend Pat Collins, the caretaker at St Mary's on the Hill School. I decided that I should be there and the principal Liz Nolan kindly collected me at home. It was a lovely occasion and I enjoyed being in the midst of the staff once again, all of whom had been so good to me and so supportive during my teaching years there. I knew by their good wishes and the smiles on their faces that they were happy that I was still around. But I felt as weak as water and quickly realised that I had a bit to go yet and a long road lay ahead before I would be back to my old self.

Dr Bird decided that I needed a month of rest to build up my strength before starting a course of chemotherapy, which he offered to me as a preventative measure and which I gladly accepted.

Four weeks later, and every fortnight after that, I drove to the chemotherapy unit of the Bon Secours Hospital. My treatment took most of the day to administer and I normally got home about six o'clock.

In the chemotherapy unit, about fourteen of us received our treatment at the same time, lying on our own recliners, with five nurses in charge of the administration. These nurses were the most amazing group of women I ever met. Their work was arduous. Although they were run off their feet, they never once complained or deviated from their caring and sensitive treatment of the people in their care.

Sadly, since completing the chemotherapy course, I have read in the newspapers the death notices of four patients who underwent the treatment with me. When that happens, I feel sadness, almost a personal sense of loss. A friendship and camaraderie seemed to develop among those of us who were receiving the treatment together and in that sense each loss was personal.

One of my best friends among the group was Dave Buckley, whose recliner was next to mine. Dave was a member of a northside family who were famous for their skills as barbers and I knew Dave since my teaching days in the area. His wife came from Adrigole, where my father's family lived. Once when I came home from a trip to London, I saw Dave's death in the paper. I could think of nothing else all day long only that he was gone.

On the recliner on the other side of me was one of the bravest people I have ever met. As far as I know, he is still fighting his battle and winning. You win a little every day you survive. As well as coping with cancer, he also suffered from diabetes and heart problems. Despite all his ailments, he was always in good humour, had an air of optimism about him and was a great conversationalist, with a wonderful capacity to live life to the fullest extent that he possibly could.

On the whole, I find that people are wonderfully supportive of those who are ill. My good friend the Cavan accordion player Martin Donohoe has a lovely system whereby he sends out a group text seeking prayers if a member of the Comhaltas family falls ill. In my case, following Martin's well-intentioned text, I got hundreds of text messages, Mass bouquets and good wishes of every sort. Each single one of them was important to me and I greatly appreciated each expression of love and concern and each played a part in my recovery.

As the months went by, especially after I had finished my chemotherapy in the middle of May 2012, I began to feel much better and stronger. I reached an important milestone when I decided to take the first tentative step towards singing and performing. I agreed to compére a fundraising choral concert in the Rochestown Park Hotel for the Douglas Tidy Towns Committee. The night went well and afterwards, now and again, I sang at the odd concert or cabaret.

In 2011, I performed at the Temple Bar Tradfest in Dublin, an annual Irish traditional music and cultural festival. I was booked to sing there again the following year but was unable to take part due to my illness. The musical director of the festival, Kieran Hanrahan of *Céilí House* fame, kindly kept a slot open for me for 2013 instead. It was the first serious prestigious engagement that I was offered since falling ill and it gave me an added incentive to make myself well again.

It turned out to be a great night. People told me my voice sounded as good as ever. Indeed, some people say that there is an added quality to it now that wasn't there before. In this regard, I want to pay a special tribute to Dr Bird, whose care and expertise has been largely responsible for this.

Looking back, I feel that the entire experience of dealing with cancer has enriched my life. Now, I appreciate life much more, every new day is a gift from God. Every new day is special whether it is wet or dry, hot or cold, calm or stormy and arrives to be cherished and lived to the full.

Seán singing with Martin Donohoe, the famous Cavan box player, at the Temple Bar Trad Festival in 2010. Courtesy Press Office, Fleadh Cheoil na hÉireann, Cavan.

I have a keener awareness of the love and support of Eileen and my family, my relatives and friends. In Eileen's case it seemed as if she put her own life on hold during my illness and with every fibre of her being willed me back to good health. That is love, selfless love. I am indeed a lucky man!

Seán with Paul McGrath in June 2004 at the Rochestown Park Hotel, Cork. COURTESY MIKE ENGLISH.

17

Back on Track

Today, I still perform at concerts and festivals and occasionally on radio and television. I tour abroad, mainly in England and America. Above all else, I love to sing with Comhaltas Ceoltóirí Éireann. Even though I no longer tour with Comhaltas on their *Echoes of Erin* tours because of the length of the journeys involved, I still perform quite a lot with them in Ireland. My role might vary from singing for a group of Mexican business people to acting as compére at the annual Congress Concert at the group's headquarters, Cultúrlann na hÉireann in Monkstown in Dublin.

The performance and excellence of the Comhaltas musicians, singers and dancers, who deserve much of the credit for making Irish music popular all around the globe, inspire me no end. Although they take their music seriously, there is always a great element of fun and enjoyment in their performance, maybe because they play for the love of their music and are not dependent on it for their bread and butter.

No doubt professional musicians also enjoy their music, but underlying it is the fact that they rely on it for their living and that can produce its own stresses.

Of course, I am in awe of what the present generation of professional groups produce. For individual performances, I would place the inimitable Christy Moore right at the top of the pile. I enjoy him so much that I would happily go to see him seven nights a week. Here in Cork, I always enjoy the performances of my good friends John Spillane and Mick Flannery.

In recent years, I've attended the Cork Singers' Club, which is headed up by Jim Walsh and William Hammond. The members meet every Sunday night in An Spailpín Fánach, a Cork pub famous for live music. All kinds of songs and singers are welcome. There is only one golden, unbreakable rule; no musical accompaniment of any kind. A cappella singing is, I think, the term used to describe it.

Another singers' club I visit from time to time is based in a unique rural pub, O'Sullivan's in the village of Killea near Templemore in County Tipperary. The owner is Seán O'Sullivan, a man of imposing physique, and he hosts a singers' night once every month. Singers come from all over the county and beyond. I have been there nights when over forty people would sing. I was introduced to the venue by Seán's brother Bernard who is attached to Comhaltas head office and we have become very good friends.

By and large, Irish traditional music has made significant progress during my lifetime. Today, it's played in the four

Seán gives an open-air performance in Cavan town centre for Fleadh Cheoil na hÉireann 2010. COURTESY PRESS OFFICE, FLEADH CHEOIL NA HÉIREANN, CAVAN.

corners of the earth. There are many aspects to Irish traditional music from *sean-nós* to progressive and experimental groups. Yet, almost all of them value and respect the music, so much so that the tradition is constantly evolving and moving forward in a positive direction. Indeed, if traditional music, like any other form of art, ceased to evolve and grow, it would become stagnant and fail.

Obviously, singing has been a huge part of my life. The first thing that a singer should realise – and I am certainly very conscious of it – is that singing is a God-given gift and that nobody can take credit for a good voice. I was fortunate to have been given a good, natural voice by my Maker and I was also lucky that both my parents, in their own way, nurtured and encouraged me. Many of the songs my father taught me are still in my repertoire. And I was also fortunate to go to Coláiste Íosagáin, where I learned a wonderful collection of songs, which in turn I was able to pass on to my own pupils at school. Another huge influence in my life was John T. Horne, who trained my voice. Without his coaching, I certainly would not be still singing today.

The recording of '*An Poc ar Buile*' was the other stroke of extreme good fortune to come my way. It is indeed a truly extraordinary song. Even though I recorded it more than fifty years ago, I dare not leave it out of a concert. It can still be heard on radio now and again and I am sometimes called 'The Pucker', mostly in Cork city. '*An Poc ar Buile*' has brought me to parts of the world I would never have seen and so I have to say God bless you Dónal Ó Mulláin.

Sometimes, people ask me how I can still put feeling into songs I've been singing for decades, such as '*An Poc ar Buile*' or '*Bhí Bean Uasal*'. Even though I've sung '*Bhí Bean Uasal*' thousands of times, it's still one of my favourite songs because it has a good story and a beautiful melody. When I sing it at a house party or a concert, I go back first of all to the great commandment of singing a ballad, which is to remember that a

Seán with his good friends Munchin O'Connell (*left*) and John O'Shea, the Singing Fireman, (*right*), at a reception hosted by the Mayor of Bantry Cllr. Mary Hegarty in June 2012.

ballad is a story set to music. The story of a song is much more important than the tune. The tune is there to support the lyrics. The more I immerse myself in the story, the easier it becomes for me to sing the song with passion, as everything seems to fall into place once I focus on the story. The ornamentation comes in at

Seán and fellow musicians lend a hand during the launch of the Bandon Music Festival at Guinness House, (*l–r*): Ger Murphy from the band Natural Gas, Seán, Eoin Verling from The Fushia Band, Jennifer Curtin PRO, Mairtin deCogoin from The Fushia Band, and Tim O'Riordan from Natural Gas. COURTESY IRISH EXAMINER.

the right time to support the story and I never over-ornament once I concentrate totally on the words.

In concert, being able to see the audience helps, especially if people in the audience engage with me; it's as if they are willing me to sing well. If I see satisfaction on their faces and realise that they too are part of the experience, I am encouraged to raise my performance even more.

Another important element to performing is the accompaniment, as that too helps me sing at my best. Without a shadow of a doubt, Seán Ó Riada was the best accompanist I ever had, which is extraordinary because sometimes great musicians don't make great accompanists, as they must sacrifice their own performance to allow the singer scope to interpret the song.

In my time, I've met many fine accompanists, among them the guitarist Jim Murray from Macroom, who recently gave me one of the best accompaniments I ever got when I sang '*Cnocáinín Aerach Cill Mhuire*' for a TG4 television show, *Seán Ó Sé – An Pocar.* Another fine accompanist is the Dublin harpist Mary Kelly and I was delighted that the Sligo Fleadh Cheoil of 2014 honoured her for her services to Irish music.

Down through the years, I have been blessed with great accompanists and I am grateful to each and every one. But, when all is said and done, Seán Ó Riada was the main man. Without him I would have accomplished little. It is a happy coincidence that today I have the good fortune to sing a lot with his son Peadar.

18

THE PARTING WORD

No matter where in the world I go, I enjoy nothing better than to return to my native village of Ballylickey and to nearby Bantry.

Despite the passage of time, Bantry and its hinterland has retained all its old charm, in particular the beautiful coastal scenery of the Beara Peninsula, which continues to attract tourists in their droves. The town boasts some fine hotels, guesthouses and restaurants, old and new, and hosts prestigious cultural events, such as the annual Chief O'Neill Irish Music Festival, organised by the Bantry branch of Comhaltas. Ballylickey is also a mecca for tourists. Situated at the most easterly inlet of Bantry Bay at the mouth of the Ouvane River, it is home to the very fine Sea View House Hotel and Manning's Food Emporium, listed in *The Irish Times* '100 Best Shops in Ireland'.

Recently, I went on one of my many 'down memory lane' trips to Bantry. As I rambled around the big town square, which is now a modern urban plaza, graced by striking sculptures of St Brendan the Navigator and Theobald Wolfe Tone, I recalled standing on that very spot as a child, watching with delight the famous trooping of the colours ceremony and shouting excitedly at my uncle, 'Uncle Mort! Your cap is on back to front!'

I walked up William Street to the Old Town Hall. Here again, memories came racing back. Looking up at the old, tall building, I thought of all the live shows I had seen there; the Shakespearian plays staged by the famous Anew McMaster theatrical company and the fit-ups, travelling variety shows, which always enthralled me. I sometimes think it may be here I got the urge to become a singer.

I retraced my steps back down William Street. Swains' shop, where my mother used to buy her knitting wool, is now a computer outlet. It seems like only yesterday that my sister Maureen and I went from shop to shop with my mother on a Saturday afternoon and later enjoyed a luscious jelly ice cream in Pat Murphy's in New Street. That was always one of the highlights of our week.

Then I drove out to Ballylickey to my childhood home, where I had an appointment with a television crew. They wanted to film a clip in the house where I grew up. The owners of the house, the Craigie family, kindly give us permission to film inside. I felt happy at the thought of returning to the home of my childhood.

All was going well until I was asked to do a shot walking down the stairs. As I stood on the landing, I suddenly noticed a chip on the stairs, about half-way down the banister. That notch has been there since the night my father's coffin was brought down the stairs all those decades ago.

I never did get over the sudden death of my father. It marked me for life and the shock of his unexpected passing stayed with me ever since. It left me with a huge insecurity about human life. As a result, every night I came home from a gig, no matter how late, I always made sure that Eileen and the children were still in the land of the living. Indeed, in my efforts to prove that they were still to the good, I often woke them up.

Then, as I dwelt on the loss of my father, I thought of Seán Ó Riada. Sometimes I feel I can almost hear him talking with enthusiasm about his latest musical project. Family meant everything to him too.

One night, after we arrived back in Cork from a trip to Dublin, Seán had intended driving on to Coolea himself. But we found his car had a flat tyre and so I drove him home. When we pulled up outside his house, he turned to me and said, '*Go raibh maith agat, a bhuachaill. Bhfuil fhios agat cad iad na trí nithe is luachmhaire ar domhan? Do bhean féin, do chlann féin agus teacht abhaile chucu.*' In English, this means, 'Thank you very much boy. Do you know the three most precious things on earth? Your own wife, your own family and to return home to them.' With that, he took a long pull of his cigar, gathered his belongings and said goodnight.

Looking back, life has indeed been good to me. My childhood in Ballylickey was normal and happy. My sister and I were lucky that we had parents who reared us well and gave us every opportunity they could to reach our full potential in life. I enjoyed my years teaching, particularly the thirteen years I spent in Knocknaheeny. I also enjoyed all the singing I did and my association with Comhaltas and the Irish traditional music scene generally.

As far as family life goes, I am particularly blessed. Seán Ó Riada was right when he listed the three most precious gifts in life. My own most precious gifts are: Eileen my wife; our family, Áine, Íde and Con; and Con's wife Caitríona and their children, Méabh, Seán and Ciara. And then, of course, there is the person who knows me longer than anybody else on this planet, my sister, Maureen.

Na trí nithe is luachmhaire ar domhan, do bhean féin, do chlann féin, agus teacht abhaile chucu.

Acknowledgements

Patricia Ahern

Whenever a song sung by Seán Ó Sé is played on the radio, it's usually followed by the words, 'And that was the great Seán Ó Sé.' For me, that says it all and so I was overjoyed when Seán agreed to put his story in print.

Working with Seán was both a privilege and a pleasure and I want to thank him most sincerely for his generosity in sharing the story of his extraordinary life with us all, for giving me the huge honour of co-writing the book and for his openness, commitment and enthusiasm. *Go raibh míle maith agat a Sheáin.*

Thanks to Seán's wife Eileen for being so welcoming always. Many thanks also to: The Collins Press for publishing the book; Grett O'Connor, director and producer of the television programme *Seán Ó Sé – An Pocar,* for introducing me to Seán; Úna and Senator Labhrás Ó Murchú for the beautiful foreword; *Irish Examiner, Evening Echo;* Gael Linn; Fleadh

Cheoil na hÉireann Cavan; TG4; and Mike English for permission to use photographs; Ciarán McCarthy for all his help with photographs; everyone who supplied images; and my sister Mary Lenihan for proofreading the text.

Thanks for all their love and support to my husband and best friend Denis and to Fiona, Michael, Brian, Cathy and Con and a special mention to my darling grandson Conor who fills my heart with joy.

Thank you all.

Seán Ó Sé

To all those who helped and supported me throughout my life and my career, I thank you. Here are just a few names:

Patricia Ahern, for her help, encouragement, patience and advice. Without Patricia there would have been no book.

The Collins Press

An Seanadóir Labhrás Ó Murchú agus a bhean Úna

Liz Nolan

Nuala Kelleher

Father Tim O'Sullivan

Peadar Ó Riada

Jim Walsh

William Hammond

Colm O'Shea

Father Seán O'Shea

Munchin O'Connell

John R. O'Shea

Bernard O'Sullivan (Comhaltas)

Bernie O'Sullivan (Beara)

Sean Higgins

Dan Coakley

John White

Val Manning

Eddie Bracken

Cathal Dunne

Tom O'Herlihy

Billa O'Connell

Pearse Murphy

Ger O'Donovan

Seán Ó Murchú

Noreen Meaney

Brid Higgison

Deirdre O'Shea

John Murphy

Tomás Ó Maoldomhnaigh

Peadar Forbes

Gearóid Ó Murchú

John Greene

Mícheál Ó Riabhaigh

Mary Kelly (harpist)

Bobby Gardiner

Siobhán Ní Chonaráin

Evening Echo

Irish Examiner

INDEX

Note: Numbers in *italics* refer to photographs.